new madrid

New Madrid: A Journal of Contemporary Literature
Volume V Number 2
Summer 2010

New Madrid (pronounced *New Mad-drid*) is the national journal of the low-residency MFA program at Murray State University. It takes its name from the New Madrid seismic zone, which falls within the central Mississippi Valley and extends through western Kentucky. Between 1811 and 1812, four earthquakes with magnitudes greater than 7.0 struck this region, changing the course of the Mississippi River, creating Reelfoot Lake in Tennessee and ringing church bells as far away as Boston.

The editors invite submissions of poetry, fiction and creative non-fiction. **Please note: We accept online submissions ONLY.** All submissions must be sent via Submission Manager, which can be accessed from our website. Submissions should be in MS Word format with a 12-point font, such as Times New Roman or Arial. The attachment should end with ".doc" in the file name. Submissions will be accepted only during two reading periods: Jan. 15 to March 15 and Aug. 15 to Oct. 15. Check our website for specific guidelines and announcements of special issues.

Website: *www.newmadridjournal.org*

Subscriptions: $15.00 annually for two issues.

Please send subscription requests to:

The Editors, *New Madrid*
Department of English and Philosophy
Murray State University
7C Faculty Hall
Murray, KY 42071-3341

Front Cover: Robert Dafford Murals, *George Rogers Clark*, from Paducah "Wall to Wall," Portraits from Paducah's Past

Back Cover: Robert Dafford Murals, *The First Log Cabin*, from Paducah "Wall to Wall," Portraits from Paducah's Past

Cover Images provided by Paducah Convention & Visitors Bureau and reprinted by permission of Robert Dafford.

new madrid

EDITOR
Ann Neelon

ADVISORY AND
CONTRIBUTING EDITORS
Carrie Jerrell
Dale Ray Phillips

GRAPHIC DESIGN
Jim Bryant

ASSISTANT MANAGING EDITOR
Jacque E. Day

MFA EDITORIAL BOARD
Christine Bailey
James B. Goode
Jacqueline J. Kohl
Matt Markgraf
A.J. Morgan
Karissa Knox Sorrell
Richard Thomas
Tiffany Turner
Stephen M. Vest

PRODUCTION ASSISTANT
Pamela Miller

TABLE OF CONTENTS

Book Reviews

EDITOR'S INTRODUCTION
Ann Neelon

IN 1937, 18 INCHES of rain fell in Paducah, Kentucky, at the confluence of the Ohio and Tennessee Rivers, in a matter of 16 days. On January 21st, the Ohio River rose above flood stage (52.7 feet), forcing 27,000 residents to evacuate the city for three weeks. The weather was cold, and the fury of the waters was exacerbated by sheets of swiftly moving ice. Earthen levees did not succeed in holding the swollen river back. In an attempt to inject a note of humor in an otherwise dire story, locals will doubtless inform you that the flood waters swiftly liberated Charles "Speedy" Atkins from his pedestal in a local funeral home. Speedy, so dubbed for his alacrity at stripping tobacco, had drowned fishing in the Ohio River. When no relatives stepped forward to bury him the first time he drowned, a local mortician experimented on him with embalming fluid of his own vintage, petrifying him in the process (Speedy was later recovered as a flood victim). On February 15th, the river crested at 60.8 feet.

The Flood Wall marker at First and Broadway reads, in part, "Paducah's $8,000,000 flood wall was built by the U.S. Corps of Engineers, is twelve miles long and protects the city to a height three feet above the 1937 flood level." Although, for over 50 years, the flood wall stood as witness to the devastation of the Great Flood, the grim greyness of its testimony was moderated in 1996. In the context of its efforts to revitalize its downtown, the city commissioned Louisiana mural artist Robert Dafford to paint historically realistic murals on three-city-blocks-worth of the Flood Wall (images from the murals include those featured on the front and back covers of this issue). In "Ambassadors," Paducah citizens turn out in red jackets, white pants and straw hats to celebrate the docking of three famed river boats—the *American Queen, Delta Queen* and *Mississippi Queen*—on a single sunny day. It is easy to take the beneficence of the river in the background for granted.

Over a foot of rain fell in 36 hours in some parts of Kentucky and Tennessee on May 1st and 2nd. The Great Flood of 2010 damaged or destroyed more than 10,000 homes. It also exacted 29 victims. Some died in kayaks on rapidly rising water. Some died in cars when bridges washed out. Some died in cars stuck in traffic on I-24 and inundated when the Cumberland River spilled over its banks. Some died in homes as they were washed away (two of the victims were handicapped, and their relatives couldn't rescue them due to flash floods). One man, a very lucky one, escaped with his life after a sinkhole in Jackson, Tennessee opened up and swallowed his car. The most surreal sight might have been that of a portable classroom from Lighthouse Christian School in Nashville floating down I-24 alongside hundreds of submerged cars.

For me, the physical damage that most hit home was the five million gallons of water in the basement of the Schermerhorn Symphony Center in Nashville. The Schermerhorn is a stately neoclassical building modeled after the shoebox design of such halls as the Konzerthaus Berlin and the Concertgebouw in Amsterdam. Its double-paned clerestory windows allow natural light to filter in without any sacrifice in acoustical quality. There's a *trompe-l'oeil* feel about the windows—their laminated panes, three and two inches thick, blend right into the wall. Chandeliers drip with bulbs in the shapes of pearls (river pearls are big business in Tennessee).

Other iconographic motifs include irises (the iris is the Tennessee state flower) and coffee beans (Maxwell House coffee made its debut in the Maxwell House Hotel in Nashville). Flooding in the basement might not sound too bad if you don't know that in only two hours the concert hall can be converted into a ballroom with a parquet floor. The feat of removing the seats is accomplished via amazing hydaulics located in the basement. Also in the basement is the console for the $2.5 million Schoenstein pipe organ. As Brian Bostick, senior director of communications for the Schermerhorn, put it, "The brain of the organ has essentially been disabled." A month before the devastation occurred, I accompanied a bus full of middle-school band students to the Schermerhorn to hear Wynton Marsalis. I had felt like I was exposing them to two of the wonders of the world, at least one of them relatively permanent.

Sometimes even bureaucratic language can be compelling, such as in these directives from Metro Nashville Public schools:

- Students who have been displaced from their homes and currently reside elsewhere are allowed to remain in their current school regardless of where they reside now, even if it is outside of Davidson County.
- Students who lost their standard school attire should not be expected to meet the district's guidelines immediately upon returning to school.
- Students who have been displaced from their homes will now qualify for free/reduced-price meals.
- Students who lost textbooks in the flood will not be held responsible for payment of those books, but lost books should be reported to the school for proper documentation.
- Absences for students who are absent because of the floods will be marked as excused.

Some fields in Kentucky and Tennessee are still underwater. By most estimates, at least half of the corn and a good bit of the wheat and soybeans will need to be replanted. Shipments of fertilizer will be delayed due to the railroad ties that will have to be replaced.

Elvis, evacuated from the 10 feet of water in Opryland's Wax Museum of the Stars, may qualify as the Great Flood of 2010's answer to Charles "Speedy" Atkins. He has been separated from his guitar. Recovery will be a matter of getting it back in his hands.

I owe a debt of thanks to Rosemarie Steele of the Paducah Convention and Visitors Bureau for permitting us to use images from the Flood Wall murals on our cover and for serving as a liaison with artist Robert Dafford. My gratitude also goes to MFA interns Christine Bailey, James B. Goode, Jacqueline J. Kohl, Matt Markgraf, A. J. Morgan, Karissa Knox Sorrell, Richard Thomas, Tiffany Turner and Stephen M. Vest. It is largely thanks to their commitment, hard work and literary aptitude that this issue sees the light. This issue also stands as testament to the organizational genius of Jacque Day. In fact, I see her as its prime mover.

The Typewriter (novel excerpt)
Martin Roper

KATHERINE SPENDS MOST of her time in the IBM building on
Pembroke Road although sometimes she has to do Burlington. Every day
she walks into town and crosses the river to the Southside. She wears a
navy skirt and a navy jacket and a white blouse. Flat black shoes to play
down her height. No jewellery. Nothing that is in any way telling. At least
nothing visible. Privacy is her defense. She wears beautiful, expensive
underwear. At least it is expensive to her. There is always more expensive,
her father used to say, more expensive but not necessarily more tasteful.
Money doesn't buy taste, he was fond of saying. She likes her underwear to
fit her well. When she leans forward to type at her desk in IBM she likes
to feel her knickers tighten on her a little. She likes to be reminded of
the womanliness she hides from the world. Sensuality is buried in her, not
that she would use such a word; its eroticism carries with it an affectation.
Words are forever killing the thing described.

In IBM, her goal is to remain invisible. She is good at being invisible.
No, that is not what she is, she is more like a mirror. She reflects people
back to themselves. She is as good with women as she is with men. It is a
gift she got from her father. It is the art of talking about nothing and lacing
the nothing-talk with the well-placed compliment. She is unthreatening
to the women in IBM and she pays the men just enough attention so that
they know they are men and that this business they do is serious business.
IBMers are a serious lot, a well-educated lot. Little Leo Corrigan told
her that the business of business is business and when he said that she
looked up briefly at the tiled ceiling above them as if she needed to think
it through, to absorb its weight. She nodded appreciatively as she did at
all his offerings. Leo Corrigan has red hair and smokes cigars and likes to
share these gems with her. It is his way of acknowledging that she is more
than a typist, and that he is preparing her for the future. IBM is suffused
with futurism while its very enormity ensures it remains locked in the old-
fashioned past. Katherine is indeed not just a typist. She is a DEP-er, a data
entry professional. Lord protect us from the Americans and their acronyms.
The first step towards annihilation is acceptance of the destruction of
language.

Her parents and sister were killed by the first bomb, the one in Parnell
Street. Eleven were killed in that one. Her father was talking to a man he
had bumped into outside the chipper—he was always bumping into people
he knew. Her mother was standing in front of the petrol pump belonging
to the garage. That pump was closed. Only the one across the road was
working and the boy operating that pump saw her father nod and walk
towards her mother, laughing. Mammy was watching for Siobhán to come

out of Lucky Duffys. Her mother would have taken it all in, she should have been a detective with the eyes she had. Good eyes and a good memory is all you need in this life. Mr. Duffy walked around the shop counter to take a look at Siobhán in her new shoes. She had bought her communion outfit that day and she insisted on wearing the shoes. She was pig-headed that way, Siobhán was. Her mother would have been annoyed at her for insisting on wearing them. They'd get filthy dirty, Mammy would have said.

Daddy was blasted back into the garage. A chunk of the car engine went into his chest. Mammy was blown into Tyrrell's shop. The back handle of the green Hillman motor car door hit Siobhán in the face and that was what killed her. The front door handle of the car ended up on Lucky Duffy's shop floor. Lucky Duffy is the only shop from that time still in business after all these years. Everything is changed these days on Parnell Street, what with the Blacks and the Chinese moved in. Everything is changed except the musty smell of poverty. Little Africa they call it. They wish. They wish it had such exotic flair. The first bomb went off just before half past five. Katherine was walking home from IBM. She was late because she stopped in Parsons book shop to have a quick look. She bought a book of poems by a fellow called Cavafy. She paused on the bridge and looked down at the canal water and at the red-faced knackers drinking on the bank. How happy they seemed. CIE were on strike and there were no buses in the city. Everyone was walking home and the weather was mild and she liked watching people. She liked that she fitted in as a worker. She liked that she looked professional even if the job was stupid and would be forever stupid. She was walking over the Matt Talbot Bridge when a man told her they were bombing Dublin and she looked at him like he was insane. She looked up in the sky for planes. For some reason she thought he meant there was an air-raid on Dublin. Her father used to love talking about the accidental bombing of the North Strand by the Germans during the Second World War. There were no planes in the sky. The sky was blue and there were clouds without the weight of rain in them drifting over Dublin. Then she heard the sirens.

Years later there will be an inquiry. It will be called the Barron Report and it will name everyone involved and it will establish nothing. For Katherine, naming things, though, matters. Before Parnell Street was Parnell Street, England had named it Great Britain Street. Katherine marvels at the simplicity of subjugation. How strange it must have been to walk streets with names that did not belong but were forced into belonging. Katherine studies semiotics. Thrilly willys. A little semiotics is more than enough for any life.

When she gets home that Friday night on May 17th, the night of the
bombings, she closes the door of the flat, takes her shoes off, and puts the
kettle on the cooker. She is shaking. She watches the flame under the
kettle burn and die. She goes out into the hall and puts two bob in the gas
meter. It's quiet in the hallway, no sound from the Flanagans' flat. There's
usually the dog barking or Mrs. Flanagan screaming: *Take me out of it!* She
goes back in to the flat in and puts a light to the hissing gas. She knows her
parents went out with Siobhán to get her her communion dress. She knows
where they would be shopping. She makes the cup of tea and sits down on
her bunk bed. She thinks of going down to May Byrnes and getting some
tomatoes and ham and making some sandwiches for their tea but that
would mean going out and she doesn't want to go out because as long as she
stays in the flat it means they were alive.

By nine o'clock she knows it must be bad. People say no news is good
news. This is more nonsense she has learned. No news, more often than
not, is bad news delayed. They were never out so late. Even if they were
stuck somewhere she knew her father would get through to her. Her father
would not allow anyone to keep him from getting through to his eldest
daughter. Katherine is his favourite. She is afraid to turn on the radio. She
sits there on the bed looking at the back window. She can see the top of the
mangle. Once she persuaded Siobhán to put her fingertips up to the mangle
rollers and then she had her sister roll her own hand through the rollers.
Even with Siobhán screaming she couldn't stop laughing. Her father would
not let anything happen to the family. He was so happy, her father. He had
a win in the Grand National again. People said there was no way Red Rum
would win two years in a row.

Strangely, in the midst of waiting, she herself is unafraid. Her fear is
about them. Sitting in the flat, she feels that she has been chosen. She
has been chosen to do something. She knows it is deep inside her. She is
certain. She is alone in the world. She has always had a certain kind of
clarity and her father was the only one who recognised it in her. Everyone
has always looked both alien and familiar to her at once. Being human has
always seemed bizarre to Katherine. It is more than bizarre, it is frightening.
We are so ugly, she said to her father. That's why we have art, he said, to try
and make up for our ugliness.

Now, sitting looking at the top of the mangle, she can sense her own
being, and that her sense of herself, is real. Maybe if she writes something
down. She can think of nothing.

Years later she will learn that David Mulholland is the name of the man who drove the green Hillman Avenger with the thousand pound bomb in it and parked it in Parnell Street. The letters D, I, A were part of the license plate of the car. Dia means God in Irish. David Mullholland died thirty-two years after the day he drove the car from Whitehall on the Southside and parked it in Parnell Street on the Northside. He died the day the Barron Report came out. It couldn't be made up, all the little facts and figures. He wiped the door handle of the car with a white handkerchief and ran across the road and up North Great George's Street. He was thirty-five the day he parked the car in Parnell Street, good-looking he was, some women said. Holding onto facts is sometimes the only thing we have to hold.

It is dark now and the tea she made sits cold in her white cup. Sirens are still going. She thinks she will type something, anything. Even when she writes rubbish she finds the sound of the typewriter soothing. The typewriter she has is called a Royal. Her father got it because they all liked James Bond and the fellow who wrote all the Bond books used a Royal. The typewriter has a ribbon in it that is black and red. She wishes she had an all-black ribbon. She never liked the red part of the ribbon. Red was the colour of wrong in school. The typewriter has bits she did not understand at first: tab and shift. When her father gave it to her she remembers he fed in a sheet of paper and she plinked down on the typewriter the letter k and it slapped the arm of the letter with a decisive mechanical click on the top of the blank page. What are you typing, her father said. Me name, she said. My name, he corrected. Then he said her name began with C not K and she said she was changing it to K, C being too common. Right, he said, when I'm calling you I'll make sure to pronounce your name with a K. She never liked the typewriter he got her. It was too bulky a contraption. It looked as important as a docked ship. When she rested her fingers on it, it felt as if it demanded something from her, something that would justify its grand existence. She just wanted a little portable thing like an Underwood but she could never tell her father that for fear of disappointing him. The Royal typewriter looked like it belonged to a professional writer and she didn't like the assumption. It looked like it needed an ashtray beside it with a cigarette burning in it, and a nice glass of golden whiskey. Crumpled pages on the floor. It looked nothing like the words in her head that she wrote with her pencil. They weren't words that she wrote. It was seeing feelings she was after.

The street is very quiet now, the work of the sirens is done. No more ambulances and no more fire engines. She types out a bit of a cummings poem she likes:

> i like my body when it is with your
> body. It is so quite new a thing.
> Muscles better and nerves more

There is a knock on the hall door. She ignores it. She stares at the unfinished bit of poem. There is another knock on the hall door. That has to be the police. Only the police would knock on the unlocked hall door. Everyone leaves the hall doors of the flats open on Clarence Street. Everyone knows that. She hears the hall door being shoved open and the noise of heavy footsteps. She stares at the door of the flat. The knock is on the Flanagans' door across the hall and not their door and she thanks God and wonders which of the Flanagans got caught in the bomb. Their door opens and quiet words are exchanged. Katherine looks for her place in the cummings poem and then there is a gentle knock on the door of the flat, the door that has become her door.

Ten Definitions Approximating Grief
Brett Foster

– for Frank Hogrebe

It's about to be born of the voice, the hysterical caller recorded
   on the emergency line.
For this reason convenience stores are dangerous, often robbed
   despite the hint of moonlight.
And the man slowly smoking that cigarette at the darkened rest stop
   off the interstate— he himself
maintains its stoic version: sparks expire across the parking lot
   as the heavy hours pass.
It haunts the moments before work, the days victimized by violent
   weather, the one-room nights.
Through the thin wall Pico della Mirandola tries to deny its existence,
   says Man, being the center of hierarchy,
is the molder of his own destiny. It suppresses the sound rain makes.
   It applauds the minor notes,
finds residence in the keys of the composer's final piano concerto.
   The theologian who accused
Tertullian of possessing "extreme and rigorous views" has never known it.
   The three-legged dog defeats its
greatest manifestation, and though absent in Hegel's *Phenomenology of
Spirit,*
   the director of Special Persons' Camp
sees it always, to see it fall away – farmhouse, roadside morning
   glory – and says there and there and there.

Bridal Cave

Brett Foster

"Strange is your image," he said, "and your prisoners strange."

They come in heavy numbers to be wed
inside the darkest recess of the Ozarks.
Geologic altars presuppose the clerks
outside the cave mouth, bundling bird seed.
She's said no to go-karts, strip malls are passé,
so between the type of place and time of year
he becomes an artificial paramour.
(Maybe they're just impulsive, who's to say?)
Summer blooms in sunken grottos. Bouquets
and pinwheels, still as pools, reassume
their glimmer in the subterranean gloom.
Descending, lovers leave the cabaret

as organ music fills the cavern. He says
a quick "I do" to the future matriarch.
After the recessional, groomsmen shark
upon bridesmaids; one stand-in wears a fez.
A swift reception's free of monograms:
one dispenses napkins, the champagne's snatched
from Coleman coolers. Portrait artists catch
tuxedos and stalactites in their frames.
Returning to the surface, he decides
he can get used to this idea, this wife.
Rice and sunlight tint her hair with new life,
this dream Eurydice smiling at his side.

Pensacola
Brett Foster

*"The Western Gate to the Sunshine State, Where Thousands Live the Way
Millions Wish They Could."* – Mayor Emeritus Vince Whibbs

This week's hurricane hits the Panhandle,
bends over end the palm trees to arches.
Their entangled fronds tread the squalling tides.

Floating from quayside through the downtown streets,
he estimates the damage like a humbled god
who ponders the inadvertent fruits of his petulance:

storm-pillaged store fronts with plywood remnants
splinting the bones of window frames, the cars
submerged but peeping out like crocodiles.

Flood water recedes and suctions the district's
cabin-crazed tourists, trapped three days indoors.
First-aid kits blotch the lawn of City Hall.

The Loving Cup
Christine Hale

AT FIVE YEARS old I didn't care about winning. Already I hated competing. But my mother needed me to get that cup. She told me it should be mine. I'd never heard of the prize until she brought it up, but the moment she did, I needed it bad. I needed—a matter of life and death in those days and for a long time thereafter—to please her.

Not to win the loving cup would have been far worse than simply failing to place first. Not winning meant a lazy, worthless, no-account shirking of what I was capable, at the very minimum, of doing. She made it obvious I could win this Best-in-Class award if I made the least degree of proper effort. I was smarter, prettier, and had better manners than any other child in the entire Anderson Street Methodist Church kindergarten.

Never mind that I didn't experience myself as any of those things. In my experience, I got wrong or didn't understand an alarming number of things; and she routinely told me I was ugly because my mouth turned down; and my failure at decent manners was a regular topic for correction. If my public behavior, my performance, didn't support her professed truths about me, I was simply off my form, and could have done better if I'd actually tried, and *would* have done better if I really loved her the way I claimed I did.

This situation is, I know, a so-common experience of pressured, nervous, over-achieving children. That I suffered because of it, that she made mistakes, even that she too suffered, this hardly bears examination. Suffering is common. And so is vilification of one's abusive parents, and, in memoir, the grown-up child's struggle to come to terms with the damage and the damned. What interests me here is the true nature of love, and the crooked path by which we arrive at forgiveness—or don't.

~~~

So: I am five. And she, my mother, is my You—the center of the universe, the only light I see by—and You, O beloved, have set me a single task: to win.

"Loving cup" must have been your term for the prize. Some years would pass before I'd notice that other people called the object a trophy. Nowadays I wonder if you meant to suggest the award was a cup of love, conferred on the winner by admiring adults. But at the time I understood I was to love and desire the cup itself. The "why" I did not question; your desire supplied all the motivation I needed. Soon the very words "loving cup" pulsed and gleamed with my longing for the object and all it signified. Maybe I felt way down beneath all surface forms of five-year-old knowing that if I had the cup, I'd have loving I could hold in my hands.

I can't remember one single thing about the competition itself except an oral questioning, by the head teacher, Miss Maude, of the students deemed to be in the running for the cup. The questions, I imagine now, tested our knowledge of facts kindergartners should know, such as the names of the seasons, and the president. I recall that during the questioning itself I experienced a vague contempt for how ridiculously obvious and easy the answers were. I was accustomed to knowing more answers than I was supposed to know when it came to school. I'd arrived there already knowing how to read without understanding that I did; you'd been reading to me for as long as I could remember and I'd memorized any number of Little Golden Books. How keen was my disappointment the day we received our eagerly anticipated "first books," which turned out to be mimeographed pages bearing line drawings labeled with two or three baby words. I felt distressed by how far beneath my expectations the challenge of kindergarten fell. I seemed simply to have always known things other children were learning with difficulty. Quickly I learned the price for too often having the right answer and especially for too often volunteering it—alienation from my peers. But I liked right answers: you'd taught me the pleasure that praise and approval conferred.

I don't remember if there were other categories of competition for this kindergarten Best-in-Show award. I faintly recall my fluttering terror-excitement on the big day during the hours that preceded the examination. But I recall with bitter clarity what I would carry with me, like a cup of gall, into high school and beyond: an exchange between me and some other child's mother in the anteroom just after my questioning.

Maybe I was looking smug. Maybe my reputation as smart kid and teacher's pet preceded me already at that age. Maybe I seemed like a target because I was alone; you, for some reason, were not with me as other children's mothers were. Or maybe the woman meant only to make friendly conversation with a kid who looked lonely.

She asked me if I'd studied. She might have said she bet I had. I had not. Until she mentioned it, I had no idea a person could prepare for questions; the concept of "study" was not familiar to me. I habitually read whatever I could get my hands on, including as many of the words in the *World Book Encyclopedia* as I could decipher, but that was because I liked finding stuff out. Her question brought a rush of strange feeling over me. I didn't know what it was but it had to do with the size and force of your certainty that I could and should win the prize. I swooned with fear that I wouldn't. And squirmed, at the same time, with deep shame at knowing that I probably would win, without studying, because the questions were too easy. The confusing, charged complexity of my emotions swept me away from myself.

I told that other mother a lie. I said, "My mother kept me up all night studying."

She was shocked. I was shocked. I had no idea such a thing was on its way out of my mouth; never had I told such a whopping lie. I'd be found out, and terrible punishment would follow. From that moment until the loving cup was placed in my hands, I oozed the cold sweat of fear. Misery so overshadowed winning that I barely remember the award ceremony—some end-of-year event for which I was overdressed and excruciatingly self-conscious.

Once I possessed the cup, I put it in your hands, pleasing you no end, of course. You put it on display in our house and showed it to everyone—relatives, friends, neighbors—any chance you got. If I heard you, I writhed.

The cup itself, forever poisoned by the lie, I hated. When it came to live in my room, I avoided its malevolent eye.

~~~

My mother—an abuser who'd been terribly abused; a vicious and sensitive person driven mad between twin poles of scintillating rage and catatonic despair—passed away at age 89. The following year, in the last stages of emptying the house she'd ruled and rotted in for six decades, I discovered the loving cup, furred with dust, awaiting me on a high shelf. I lifted it down reluctantly, marveling at the durable discomfort so simple an object set off in me.

I'd left home for good at seventeen, but as long as I lived there, winning awards and A's for her while losing friends and then myself in depression, drugs, and early marriage, every encounter with the loving cup's arms-akimbo handles and slender self-righteous face pained me freshly. The moment my mother's interest in it waned sufficiently, I banished it from my room to the top of the bookcase in the den, but I could not banish its effect: a blood guilt. No one ever said a word about my transgression but my secret awareness of it scourged me.

Why had I lied? At five, the lie made me feel as unworthy of winning as if I had cheated. Even in kindergarten, I had a compulsion toward truth telling, yet I lied easily and urgently, betraying my values. My values were her values, of course. *She* despised lies, *she* expected my public success, but most of all she required—in order to stay alive—I knew *that* already at five, too—my absolute loyalty. When I lied to plump myself up, to protect myself by disguising the ease with which I'd beat out my peers, I made my mother look mean. I sinned against she-who-was-my-god, and for that I sure enough expected retribution.

I couldn't trace my fear to its source at five, and not for years afterward. As far as I could get was that I had, for some reason, made myself bigger than I deserved, and that I must have a tendency to self-aggrandize under pressure, and because of that, I merited whatever criticism and misfortunes befell me. I replayed my kindergarten debacle: the social faux pas, the spontaneous moral transgression, and the baffling question of *why*, in a world I was determined to perceive as just and fair, my efforts to be good so frequently ended up as evidence that I was bad.

To make that equation balance, I compulsively generated shame and blame. On that compulsion, I built a way of being. A means of understanding myself, my mother, the duties of love, the arithmetic of life.

With a good dose of shame I could hammer myself down a few notches, making damn sure I wasn't getting swell-headed, and that I was, damn-sure, striving with maximum effort to be the kind of person—completely at the service of someone else's agenda—my mother had taught me I better be if I were to have the least chance of deserving love. I hewed a knife from shame, too. A cutter before it was the fashion, fearful of blood and observable consequence, I never put a real blade to my skin. When I thought of razors I pictured only the final solution, the laying open of my veins (I never could conceive any kind of middle ground). I needed pain, just like modern self-mutilators, to remind myself I was alive when depression ground me numb.

Shame served as shield, too. A steely show of passive-aggression toward my mother and those subsequent objects of desire—men, jobs, degrees, a perfect marriage, a published book—who took her place in my life. *I can make myself so low you will have to love me, for pity's sake.* And if you don't, then I'll just glory in decadence, grant myself license to engage fully in self-destruction via black moods, suicidal ideation, and drug addiction. It never occurred to me in those days that this behavior, seeking death through incremental self-neglect rather than grand gesture, *exactly* replicated hers.

Lastly, paradoxically, shame gave me a way to stay alive. Even as I courted death and wallowed self-pityingly in my miseries, the essence of me, quick-witted and lively, found a way to survive by gaming the shame. *I'll do it to myself before you can do it to me.* This way, I'd never have to be surprised by disaster or rejection, never be caught out trusting anyone or anything that might betray me. I'd expect the worst, and expect it so good I could never be blind-sided.

The problem with this winning strategy was, of course, that it made me want to die. But for years I managed despair with some success, via an ever-shifting mix of magical thinking and self-medication. Sometimes, of course, I racked up worldly successes despite myself—often in school, sometimes in publication or love. Every time that happened, I'd catch myself compulsively dissembling to make it look harder so I could be both more special (look how hard I worked!) and more like everybody else (look how hard I *had* to work!). All the while, I'd be compulsively disassembling, too—sabotaging success by pointing out to myself and everybody else all the ways it wasn't yet *real* success. Always, more striving remained to be done.

All this—from a single lie in kindergarten. All this, without ever comprehending why I lived the way I did, suffered as I did, and wanted—so often, just like my mother—to turn my face to the wall and die.

~~~

The loving cup I could not toss out with the rest of the two-dozen extra-large black plastic sacks of detritus I carted from the house of my childhood to the curb. I carried it home with me, at that time eight hundred miles distant. That object my mother and I had so desired—a cheap, soft-metal, goblet-shaped trophy mounted on an even cheaper white plastic cylindrical base—lives now in the windowsill alongside my writing desk.

Corrosion has dulled and pitted the loving cup's once brassy face, blurring the words engraved there. I make myself make them out sometimes, a kind of penance for the genesis of my grasping at affirmation and belonging, and my prickly relationship to the truth about myself and other people.

Lucy Hale

says the cup, insisting on a first name I abandoned in first grade, twenty years before my parents reluctantly stopped addressing me that way.

1961, A.S.M.C. Kindergarten

it taunts me, naming and dating that first social setting in which I blatantly failed to fit in.

Honor Award

it mocks me, reflecting back a quality I have wanted to exemplify
and yet repeatedly betrayed,
often in the very same moment,
all my life.

Not just self-perception but my path has circled and collapsed, repeatedly, inside the loving cup's steep and slippery walls. I lied about my mother on the way to winning the cup she needed. Inside my blurted untruth nested truth I needed to tell, feared to know, and had no words for anyway: she did have that kind of power over me and, to my shame, she did exercise it inexorably.

She was my very first You. The mirror that defined me, at five. It's no wonder I confused my honor with her necessity. I balled my fists, stood my shaky ground, and spit a mouthful of the fire that consumed me—at someone, that ignorant or innocent or lamely curious other mother, who had no idea what a puzzle she was looking at.

The loving cup in my window shows me what faced her then: a desperate and angry small girl beating herself bloody against the first in the lifetime series of desirings I would mistake for the true practice of love. My mother is ten years gone, and a mother myself now for more than twenty, I see her finally by my light. Angry, desperate, beaten, she confused me with the thing she needed and would never have: a cup of love she could hold in her hands. ▰

Amen and Amen

Julie L. Moore

I'm sitting on my front porch
    by an open window. The breeze,
        tinged with the copper of coins,
will purchase rain by morning.

Inside, my daughter's playing the piano,
    singing Cohen's "Hallelujah,"
        her voice rising, the keys
stirring sparrows in the pine trees and maples.

I want to care about her music,

but I'm reading O'Connor, considering Displaced
    Persons, the ungodly ways we ruin one another.
        Banks have ruptured like arteries
while CEOs drink Bloody Marys.

Broke, a man kills himself in Chicago.
    On the page, the priest mentions Jesus.
        Mrs. McIntyre snaps, says Jesus doesn't belong,
damns his name. Their words

blaze like Ashley's song, like the light

glowing at our front door, drawing a moth.
    Night descends around me like a net.
        The monarchs have long since left
for Mexico. They're getting drunk on cheap

nectar and spawning larvae that slurp
    the toxic juice of milkweed.
        Their cells pack on the poison like muscles.
When they burst from their chrysalis,

their wings sprout orange—loud
    and clear—proclaiming
        to every hungry predator
how terrible they taste. Hallelujah.

And other butterflies are question marks.

The single, pearly punctuation etched
    on each ventral surface like a hieroglyph.
      Their curvaceous wings silhouettes
of every explanation we seek.

Pain is my appendage again.

(Surely, I've done this before.) Sutures
    from my sixth surgery sting. Within
      the house, my husband calls the dog,
his command wafting through the screens.

Maggie scratches her ear, her tags
    jangling like the crickets. Ashley sings on
      as though her breath's no longer her own,
absorbed now in benediction. Our amen un-

broken, like a world without end.

The lion of this March
Julie L. Moore

devoured two 20-year-olds,
the children of dear friends,
from two families.

One, Plath-like, by imbibing
gas, the helium lifting him
beyond this world—

his, the sixth funeral for suicide I've attended.

(All the names swirl in my head,
whirring like the wings of gnats—
Michael, Vancil, Teresa, Phil, Ryan, Peter.

Death, it seems, makes no one special.)

The other, in Tennessee,
by her own hand, yes, but by accident,
falling asleep as she drove—

and oh, what bloody dreams
do come!—the turn of the wheel
screwing her into a tree.

Go, March, go, please go out
like a lamb. And as you leave,
carry on your small and blemished back

all the grief you can bear.

Waiting Room
Julie L. Moore

You sit in the waiting room as the old farmer speaks
the doctor's name like any other name. Like normal.

I hear he's good, the hospital receptionist replies.
I've met him. He seems like the nicest guy.

And once again, you sit with your tongue
locked behind your teeth.

You've kept quiet for years
since she asked you to (his ex-

wife, that is), afraid as she was for her own
life. But your thoughts grow

loud as banging pots, your memory howls like a dog
eyeing an intruder. You know the real

story. How her upstanding doctor-
husband slapped her through all seven

pregnancies. How he delivered the babies
himself to hide the bruises

at home. Punched like pillows
their kids in the garage. Shaped

with his own skilled hands
his oldest son, landscaper extraordinaire, well-mannered

hunter of neighborhood girls,
molester of his sisters.

You remember the phone call.
When she told you her son dreamed of touching

your daughter. You steel yourself.
Carve out a room inside yourself where you wait.

Fingering words like sterile instruments.
Stroking their sharp edges.

Out of Love Poem
Sandra Kohler

The porch. My birthday month. So what
if there are cherries along with chocolate
every night, it's autumn. It's the first day
of August and already I have heard crickets,
glimpsed a heron, watched flocks of blackbirds
materialize toward dusk like a storm low
in the eastern sky, swirl and scatter, vanish.
My sick husband heals. Lovemaking returns.
Will love? Can I make my life something
I love? I love it so much that even when
I'm out of love with it I can't not want it.
Like a husband angry at his wife who turning
over in bed is filled with an involuntary
shudder of desire for her, like a wife mad
at her husband who lying next to him feels
her nipples harden as they brush his warm
back. In my dream I have my arm in my
husband's but hold the hand of the man
on my other side. I realize this is what I
want, what women want, both men. Who
we are and how we see ourselves is fragile,
mutable, fractal, unfinished. All our wishes
have dark sisters, our dreams nightmare
daughters and sons. Anyone can revise
the past; the present's intractable, future
incalculable. I can toast bread and brew
coffee, bring it to my husband, I can cut
flowers for the house, put them in our
bedroom, study, on the dining room
table. I can't change what's coming.
I can only try not to impose a scrim
of wish and will between my mind
and all that it touches.

To Texas

Sandra Kohler

Along all the roads in northcentral Pennsylvania
banks of Black-eyed Susan, coneflower, cosmos
are shrinking, thwarted, sere. In my garden yellow
evening primrose are drying out, dying, even
the stubborn zinnias are wilting. Autumn in July,
seven inches below average rainfall for the year
so far. The promised storms don't come. I am
flat, empty, dry, barren. None of this verbiage
will give my roots water. Rain is a desert mirage,
illusion which approached, vanishes. I dream we
are moving to Texas: a Texas of mind, parched
place, to which we've been exiled this summer.
The brown fields along the creek, the alley
are our Texas. In another dream I'm watering
the parched zinnias I should have thinned when
they sprouted. I was greedy, wanted them all
to bloom, left them to fight for life. In the dream
they've thinned themselves, each drying stalk
a skeletal emblem of earth's ruin. Flushed by
this weather, rattlesnakes are coming down
out of the mountains, the Daily Item proclaims
on its front page. What will come will come.

Selves
Sandra Kohler

The light from the southeast is tender, faintly
warm, pale rose against the dove grey smudge
of fog over the hills, the river's risen spoor.
Dreaming, a crowd of women in my house,
sister, aunt, grandmother, speaking a language
I don't understand, rebuke my failure to respect
their customs, obey their authority, then fall to
quarreling among themselves. The cloud of gold

leaves below my neighbor's garage hovers in light
as if it could float off, echoed by a tree beyond
the creek, distant sister. I am distant from all
my sisters. The trees taking in November's mild
arrival hold their colored leaves like breath.
Stillness. Nothing stirs before me, though behind
my back a man is putting on clothes, breathing
hard, grunting a little. What am I learning in

struggling dreams, engraving in memory? How
do we learn to accept the gestures of an alien
culture as they are meant, rather than as we
see them? The misgiven gift, the slight intended
as kindness. Wanting to be seen as we are is
wanting to be seen as we see ourselves, known
as we believe we know ourselves: impossible
blind demands. I am as guilty of these as anyone

I know. I am all my dream's women, sister,
aunt, niece, mother, daughter: angry wounded
wounding selves. The night is an alternate
narrative, its own story that becomes memory,
engraved as experience in cells that do not
distinguish between dream and day, imagined
and sensed. There is something frightening
in this, something false, something true.

A Flowery Tale
Beth Lordan

MRS. CROWLEY WAS just letting herself down onto the worn green plastic of the third chair in the lobby when Denise came out of the office with a young woman carrying a pot of flowers. "The elevator's right there," Denise said. She had the dinner menu in her hand. "She's on the ninth floor, apartment 912—turn to your left when you get off."

The blossoms were strange looking, like yellowish lettuce leaves, but the woman had a sweet face, and 912 was the apartment where Mr. Jessup had died two weeks ago; these three facts struck Mrs. Crowley as interesting, especially coming all together that way, although they didn't all come together for her until well after the woman had disappeared into the elevator. Mrs. Crowley was ninety, after all, and things struck more slowly than they once had, but she straightened her walker in front of her and settled back with a small smile: remembering who had moved into Mr. Jessup's apartment would fill the slow time until dinner very nicely, and made it worth the trouble she'd taken to be up from her nap and down here before four o'clock.

Denise tacked the menu in the little case they had for it and clicked the little door shut. "Ham and scalloped potatoes," she announced, and went back into the office and closed the door.

"Ham and scalloped potatoes," Mrs. Crowley repeated in her dreamy voice. "Tidings of comfort and joy."

~~~

In 912, Estelle turned the dark green pitcher of forsythia branches a quarter way around, wiped a bit of pollen off the table, and went to the bathroom and combed her hair, which was a wreck. Then she went back into the sitting room and, as she'd hoped would happen, all the things she'd done to make it pretty came at her at once and she could see it whole. The curtains she'd made from a pale green stripe hung straight and looked fresh, the two easy chairs sat at an inviting angle to the coffee table and the couch, and nobody could have guessed that the dark green throw pillows weren't really silk. The forsythia looked a little spindley, but everything else was just about perfect. In the bedroom, down the short hall, everything was still a jumble: towels and sheets sitting on the bed, the black plastic bag erupting from the laundry cart, her clothes on their hangers draped over the dresser—everything just where the moving men had set it down—but she'd get to that after she'd had a cup of coffee and her sweet roll. She'd been so busy she hadn't really had lunch, just a hard-boiled egg, and she needed something to tide her over to dinner, which she'd decided she'd have downstairs in the dining room, but for the last time. Now that she had the one-bedroom, after a year stuck in the little efficiency while her name rose slowly on the waiting list, she intended to live like a normal person instead of like somebody practicing to be dead. She was only seventy-four, and from now on until she was too weak to do it, she'd cook her own dinner every night.

Not that people weren't friendly here, in a casual way. This morning, when she went down to the lobby hoping to find out what dinner was going to be, Mrs. Linster came down the ramp with her cane and said, *Good morning—this is your moving day, isn't it?* and Mr. Phillips said, *Cold day for it*, just as if moving from Building A to Building B involved going outdoors. They weren't particular friends—Estelle had made no particular friends—but she said back, *It'll be a full day's work*, and they had agreed. There had been no mail in her box, and the menu for tonight hadn't been posted yet, and Mr. Phillips had said, *Seems like it must be about time for pot roast again—nothing like pot roast on a cold day*, but Mrs. Linster said, *I doubt it—we're due for ham again.* Mr. Phillips chuckled as if someone had been witty, and said *Oh, ham, and those green beans they cook to mush—you got to wonder what that dietician they've got thinks about, meals like that for a bunch who all got high blood pressure.*

Estelle smiled, pouring the water into the coffee maker. The poor old coot thought he was being flirtatious, another widower hoping to remarry, to get somebody to cook for him while he could still eat and sit by his bed while he died. She'd been that second wife already, thank you; Bill Hennessey had been a good man, and her life as Mrs. Hennessey had been easier in many ways than when she was married the first time, to Paul LeTourneau, and worked beside him in their small store for thirty years until he dropped dead one Tuesday while she was weighing out ground beef. Life goes on, she reminded herself, washing and drying her four blue coffee mugs, and regret is a waste of time. She had a new home now, and a new life, she reminded herself, though exactly what that new life was going to consist of once she got unpacked and settled she'd rather not consider, so when her doorbell rang just after she'd put three of the mugs into the cupboard and closed the door, she was glad of the distraction. She wasn't expecting anybody, but people did sometimes stop to borrow or offer something, and the building's security required that outside visitors be buzzed in, so she answered the door without even peeping through the peephole.

What she saw first was the pot of tulips, apricot-colored and ruffled, and they reminded her swiftly that she'd meant to have something that color in her sitting room, which had turned out so well already—it seemed, in that first moment, barely possible that these flowers, these quietly flamboyant miracles, were meant for her, a housewarming gift. And so the voice in which she said, "Yes?" might have been less peremptory than usual, even though the old bitter wariness hovered nearby, its familiar shelter ready: once in Building A the delivery person had brought Mrs. Bradshaw's monthly flowers to Estelle's door by mistake (lilies, they had been, and the scent had lingered half the day) and here it was happening again in Building B—you'd think they'd learn to read.

But: "Mrs. Hennessey?" the woman carrying the flowers said, though tentatively, as if she, too, suspected there'd been a mistake. She looked to be in her late thirties, dark-haired and ruddy-cheeked, with those little ugly glasses people wore now.

"Yes?" This woman wasn't a delivery person, and these tulips weren't from the grocery store, with that thick tissue paper rising up around the pot instead of tacky gold foil.

"Mrs. Hennessey, I'm Janet Northrup—well, Janet Keyes now, but I was Janet Northrup when I was with you." She smiled, pretended a small laugh. "Oh, I suppose there were so many of us, and it *has* been almost thirty years, but I was at the university in Livingstone for a meeting, and I thought, Janet, you just drive over to Clayborne and see if you can't find Mrs. Hennessey, and tell her thank you."

The memory came onto Estelle all of a piece, how one afternoon ten years ago (it was July, the windows open, she'd been married to Bill Hennessey for just nine days and he was upstairs having his rest), while she was sweeping that peculiar kitchen floor in her new home, she heard a car pull up and stop, and when she walked down the dim hall there stood a fellow in a loose Hawaiian shirt, the blues and reds vivid even in the shade of the front porch. He peered through the screen as she came, and when she said *Yes?* he said, *I was looking for Mrs. Hennessey. I'm Mrs. Hennessey,* she said, and it was the first time she had used the name aloud. *I don't know,* he said. *I guess I might be mixed up,* but he was a stranger to her, she had no reason to be cruel or kind, so she said *What did you want?* Again he shrugged, scratched the back of his neck, spoke away from her. *I was looking for—a long time ago, I lived here—*

Margaret Hennessey's dead and gone, she said. *I'm Mrs. Hennessey now,* and he snapped his head back around and glared at her. *You're Mrs. LeTourneau,* he said, an accusation. *You're Frenchie's wife.* And she matched his tone, abrupt and vicious: *I was. I'm Mrs. Hennessey now,* and she closed the inside door and turned the lock and walked back to the kitchen. When she heard the car start and drive away, she took up her broom and went on with her sweeping.

She had understood then: for years Margaret Hennessey had filled her barren house with foster children, one of her many good deeds, sneaky, pale, unpleasant kids Estelle had kept a particular eye on in Frenchie's, and here was one of those children, come back. She had found the letters from them, the Mother's Day cards, graduation and birth announcements, two shoeboxes full in the bedroom closet; she had burned them, and had opened and thrown away the others that had come later.

And she understood now, standing in this new doorway, this new kitchen: after all this time, after the eight good years with Bill Hennessey and then his long last illness and his death, after she'd buried him and moved fifteen miles away, here was another one.

~~~

"I'd say she was a niece," Mrs. Crowley said. "Somebody's niece."

"Oh, for heaven's sake," Mrs. Coulter said, and gave a little rap with her cane, "what does a *niece* look like?"

The outside door slid open and Mr. Phillips came in with a trickle of the outside cold. "Nippy," he said, and blew on his gloved hands.

"They said twelve below last night," Mrs. Coulter said. "That's not nippy, that's damned cold."

"Not like a daughter," Mrs. Crowley said. "Embarrassed instead of worried?"

"Couldn't be a daughter," Mr. Phillips said. "She never had kids."

"Who are we talking about?" Mrs. Coulter said. "I thought she went to see Mr. Jessup."

"Oh, he died," Mrs. Crowley said. "Mrs. Hennessey's in 912 now."

"I don't think there's a bit more room in those one-bedrooms," Mrs. Coulter said. "Just more catchalls."

"Kitchens aren't any bigger," Mr. Phillips said.

"That's what I mean," Mrs. Coulter said.

~~~

But that fellow had been sweaty, and he hadn't brought a pot of tulips the likes of which Estelle had never seen. "Janet Northrup," she said.

Janet Northrup Keyes laughed, again, more certainly now, encouragingly, and held the flowers out to Estelle. "And you weren't easy to find!" she said. "I went to the old house first, and—well, time goes by, doesn't it?—but they didn't know a thing, and then I thought, Well, you could try the *phone* book, silly." The blowsy flowers quivered a little. The pot must be quite heavy.

Estelle had to take it. To do that, she had to open the door farther, had to step back. So she said, "Well, come in." She could explain in a moment. She accepted the pot, which was heavy, and cool, and now she could see that each bloom had a streak of pale green at its base, a blotch of brilliant yellow inside; there seemed to be a dozen of them. "These are very pretty."

"Oh, I'm glad you like them—I wasn't sure, they're so unusual, but they didn't have any yellow ones like you used to have." Janet Northrup Keyes stepped into the tiny kitchen area, rubbing the backs of her hands down her sides, a gesture that irritated Estelle vaguely, made her think of bitten nails and chapped wrists, and she turned away to set the flowers on the counter. "Anyway, you weren't listed in the phone book, so I went to the post office—I would have gone to Frenchie's store and asked there, but Frenchie's is completely *gone*—there's a convenience store there now!—and the postmaster said you'd moved over here a year ago." The coffee maker gurgled. "And then when I got *here*, the office said you were moving *today*, and I thought, well, she's not going to want company on *moving* day, but I have to go back tomorrow, and I'd already bought the flowers, and it just seemed—this is *nice*, though—it doesn't *look* like you've just moved in!"

"Well," Estelle said.

"Oh, I know!" Janet Northrup said, and then tilted her head a little to the side—yes, that was how Margaret Hennessey did when she had one of her sayings to offer—"'A plan in hand is the job half done'—right? Oh, I say that all the time to my students—I'm a teacher now!"

"My plan was a cup of coffee, before I get back to work," Estelle said. She could hardly avoid it, so she said, "Would you like a cup?"

"Oh," Janet Northrup said, who seemed to say Oh entirely too often, "if it's not any trouble—I don't want to be a bother. I just wanted to—well, you know, you were so *kind* to me—to all of us—"

"Have a seat," Estelle said, gesturing to the sitting room. She was well aware of what a kind person Margaret Hennessey had been; Margaret Hennessey had been famous for her kindness. Margaret Hennessey had also had no real sense of color—beige was what she'd done the Hennessey house in, and that awful pink bathroom; she wouldn't have appreciated these tulips one bit.

So Janet Northrup went into the sitting room and said, "Oh, what a wonderful view you have—in the fall it must be just beautiful!"

Estelle had had no choice about the view; she had taken the first available one-bedroom apartment. "So you're a teacher?" she said. She took out the second cup and tried to remember where she'd put the sugar bowl while Janet Northrup stood by the window and chattered on about her third graders and what a challenge and privilege it was to be a teacher. Estelle wondered if she'd really put on so much weight that she could be mistaken, even after probably twenty years, for Margaret Hennessey. She would set it straight in a minute. She'd carry the mugs of coffee into her pretty sitting room and she would say, *Janet Northrup, I'm sorry to tell you that your Mrs. Hennessey is long dead*. She didn't exactly *regret* how she'd told the fellow in the shirt, or not ever mentioning it to Bill. Though the fellow in the shirt had certainly been rude. "Please," she said, "have a seat."

"And it took me so long—now that I'm finally here, I can't stay long—I have to be back for a dinner," Janet Northrup said. "Oh! I was so sorry to hear about Mr. Hennessey—the man in the post office told me." She took off her coat, finally, and laid it on one end of the couch.

"He was a good man," Estelle agreed. She'd have to forego her sweet roll, since she only had the one, and she hadn't found the sugar bowl. "Do you take sugar? I don't have any milk."

"Just black is perfect. I'm trying to lose a little." She patted her middle, which was, truly, in need of some decreasing, and sat down. "You'd never believe I was such a skinny kid, would you?"

"Most of you were." It was unusual that tulips had scent, but these were sweet, even over the smell of the coffee.

"Oh!" It was almost a wail, and the coffee in the pot Estelle had just lifted sloshed. Again: "Oh!" and Estelle stared at the coffee. "I *remember* this pitcher! It's the lemonade pitcher, isn't it!"

"Is it," Estelle said, but Janet Northrup was beyond.

"Oh, I remember it so well!" Janet Northrup cried, and then she sobbed, and just like that, it was too late to tell her the facts.

Estelle had found the pitcher in the Hennessey back room. It was the only thing from Margaret Hennessey's days in the house that Estelle had brought with her, and only because she'd been so certain Margaret Hennessey hadn't had any idea how handsome it was. Apparently, though, it had been in daily use: the lemonade pitcher. She did not believe that Bill Hennessey had ever asked to have lemonade. She herself wasn't fond of it, but if he had asked, she certainly would have made it. They'd usually had iced tea with their suppers; he'd never complained.

Let this girl take the pitcher, and leave the tulips here, a fair trade. Really: was there any point at all in explaining? Janet Northrup would be embarrassed, she'd know she'd made the trip for nothing, she'd probably get all grief-stricken—ridiculous, since the woman had been dead now more than ten years—and what would she do with the flowers? Take them to the cemetery? No.

"You should take it with you," Estelle said. She put Janet's mug on the coffee table and sat in one of the easy chairs. There was no great challenge in passing for Margaret Hennessey, since the mistake was already made. People believed what they wanted to believe. She'd keep the conversation general, she'd say pleasant things about the old days in Clayborne, and Janet Northrup would never have to know. And those tulips would look glorious in here.

Janet Northrup had taken her glasses off and was digging in her purse. "Oh, I couldn't," she said.

~~~

"Seventy-five, if she's a day," Mrs. Coulter said.

"Seventy, I'd say," Mrs. Crowley said.

Mrs. Linster laughed. "You always say seventy!"

"Do I?" Mrs. Crowley said, delighted.

"It doesn't matter how old she is," Mrs. Coulter said. "What matters is *when*—you get a birthday every year anyway."

Mr. Phillips came down the ramp, zipping up his jacket. "Time for my constitutional," he said. "Any of you ladies care to join me?"

"I think she told me once her birthday was near Christmas," Mrs. Linster said.

"When is Easter this year?" Mrs. Richmond said. "Maybe Easter's early this year—tulips for Easter."

"Last chance," Mr. Phillips said.

"Don't stand there making the door stay open," Mrs. Coulter said. "It's freezing."

Mr. Phillips wrapped his scarf over his face and went out.

"Seventy was a good age," Mrs. Crowley said. "Seventy was an honor and a blessing."

"She never mentioned brothers or sisters, though," Mrs. Linster said. "I don't know where a niece would come from."

"I don't mention mine," Mrs. Coulter said, "but that doesn't mean I don't have 'em."

"I had four brothers," Mrs. Richmond said. "Allan, Brian, Ciaran, and Darren. And me, Ellen."

"It could be from her husband's side," Mrs. Linster said. "It was a second marriage for both of them."

~~~

"I insist," Estelle said.

Janet Northrup found a tissue and blew her nose. "Isn't it funny," she said, but her voice was watery, wobbly, "how such an ordinary thing will bring everything back? I mean, it's like the whole kitchen is right *here*," she said, "that whole *time*, it's right—" and then, before got her glasses back on, she was absolutely bawling. "I'm sorry," she squeaked between sobs.

Estelle knew that Margaret Hennessey would, at this moment, have moved over to the couch and put her arm around Janet Northrup. Estelle sipped her coffee, which she no longer particularly wanted, or at least wanted less than she wanted this overwrought woman out of her sitting room. She said, "Surely the old kitchen wasn't *that* bad."

"Oh," Janet Northrup wept, "oh, it was so *wonderful*—you were so *warm*," she hiccupped, "everything was so *perfect*, and it's all—gone!"

"Well, you're not gone," Estelle said. She had no intention of actually lying, so she didn't say *And I'm not gone.* "Drink your coffee. You'll feel better." And Estelle had some more of hers, as an example, she supposed.

Janet Northrup managed to blow her nose again and smile weakly, and then, obediently, she picked up the coffee mug, though her hand was shaking, and Estelle could just see coffee splattering all over the throw pillows. "I'm really sorry—I was afraid this was going to happen." She put her glasses back on and took a sip of her coffee.

Estelle said, "It's quite all right," which seemed enough like something Margaret Hennessey would say. And Janet Northrup hadn't spilled anything.

Janet Northrup sipped again, and put her mug down carefully. "That is better," she said, and took a deep breath and let it out slowly. "I think I'm all right now."

"Good," Estelle said.

Janet smiled more strongly, and touched the green jug with her fingertips. She cleared her throat. "Really, it wasn't just that I was in Livingstone. I actually come to the university pretty often, and I never tried to find you before. I came because my therapist encouraged me to."

"Ah." Estelle was looking at Janet Northrup's fingernails, which were short, polished pink, nicely shaped., which was somehow surprising. Estelle did not like the feeling it gave her.

"Yes. I started seeing her because—well, my husband wants to have children, and I *thought* I did too, but I keep—well, I don't think I'd be a very good mother." This last came out very quickly.

"I'm sure—"

But Janet Northrup held up her hand and shook her head. She kept her eyes on the jug and went on. "And my therapist says that's perfectly understandable given—what happened. What my mother did."

~~~

"Where does he *go?*" Mrs. Linster said.

Mrs. Coulter knocked her cane against the chair leg. "In and out, in and out—like an old dog," she said.

"He's a wanderer," Mrs. Crowley said. "A wanderer in the wilderness."

"He's an old goat," Mrs. Coulter said.

They laughed, even Mrs. Richmond, who hadn't heard what Mrs. Coulter said.

"You never know," Mrs. Crowley said. "There are worse things to be."

~~~

"So Ginny—my therapist—she thought if I went back to where I had felt *safe*—" She took a deep breath and let it out slowly, and Estelle felt herself short of air, and how good it would feel to do that, but surely Janet Northrup, whose mother had done something terrible, would feel mocked, so she only nodded again. "If I went back to the old house, she thought I'd see that it was just—normal. And that I would see that it wasn't—miraculous, I guess. Just something normal people normally did. So I'd know I could do it."

Distantly, Estelle noticed that she herself was nearly exhausted—no roll, no air, no rest, and all this uproar, like thunder coming rolling all the way from the Hennessey house, where Margaret Hennessey had known things Estelle did not wish to think about.

Janet, though, took a drink of her coffee, so Estelle did, too, and took her own deep breath that nearly turned into a yawn, but she held it back. "Well," she said.

Janet turned the jug of forsythia a little. "I guess *I* thought we'd reminisce, you know? I'd say remember that time you made a picnic breakfast, and remember how we all laughed when Mr. Hennessey spilled the ketchup that time, and somewhere in talking about old times you'd say something—I don't know—and everything would fall into place, and it would be *nice.*"

"There were nice times," Estelle said carefully.

Now Janet did look at Estelle, very directly, pale brown eyes with dark lashes, and Estelle knew that she'd been found out: *You're not Mrs. Hennessey*, Janet Northrup would say, *are you?* The shame was abrupt—her scalp prickled with it, her mouth went dry—Margaret Hennessey would never have done this. *You're not Mrs. Hennessey*, and what could she say back? *I meant well?*

But Janet gave a sad smile and said, "I don't think you actually remember me, do you?"

Estelle felt herself blushing, and lightheaded. She didn't dare move, but when she spoke she heard her voice softer, sadder, a voice like Margaret's, nothing of Mrs. LeTourneau in it at all. "I'm sorry," she said. "I should have said—if I had a picture—over the years there were so many—"

"Oh, I understand," Janet said. She adjusted her purse beside her on the couch and sat up straighter. "And I was only there four months. I remember Beverly had been there more than a year."

"Most of you didn't stay long," Mrs. Hennessey said. "I'm sorry my memory's so bad."

"Still. I did want to thank you. You were good to me, and I learned some important things from you that I wouldn't have learned at—from my own—parents."

"That's something." So now she'd come to lying. She should have told her straight off *You've made a perfectly understandable mistake.*

Janet nodded. "It is something. I mean, you taught me how to make a bed and how to do dishes and set the table. The first time I ever took a shower was in your house, the first time I ever went to the dentist you took me. Just—oh, *civilized* things."

"Ordinary things." She was so tired, so weary.

"Yes," Janet said. "Ordinary things. And to think about other people— you had us make cards for that family whose house burned down. And manners, and why they mattered. Oh, and about honesty. When I stole that little Santa Claus pin from Frenchie's store, and you made me take it back—that was very painful for me—no, no, I'm not saying you were wrong, not at all, I think you were absolutely right."

Janet Northrup went on, speaking of gardens and pets and lessons learned about responsibility and consequences, but Estelle was breathing the cabbage-smelling air of Frenchie's, the sharp click sound the pin had made when the girl put it on the counter rang in the empty store, and there stood Margaret Hennessey behind the little thief, her wide hands pale on the shoulders of the girl's dark winter coat, and Estelle felt in her jaw the remnant of her own weary anger, and in the back of her throat she tasted the nausea that followed it, the shame of shaming—the memory was so vivid that when Janet Northrup said, "Oh, look at the time!" and stood up, it was all Estelle could do to prevent herself from blurting *I remember you.*

Instead, she too stood, and steadied herself with her hand on the back of her chair.

"That's right," she managed to remember and say, "you've got to get to your dinner."

"Yes, and I'll be a little late," Janet said, putting on her coat, "but it was worth it—for me, I mean."

"It was nice of you to come," Estelle said, and discovered that she could, indeed, walk. She followed Janet to the kitchen. "And I never thanked you for the flowers—they're beautiful."

"Oh, you're welcome—and I'm sorry I had that spell—it was just one of those things!"

"Wait," Estelle said. "I wanted you to take that old pitcher."

"But it looks so nice here," Janet said.

"You should have it," Estelle said, but discovered that she could not smile, so she turned from Janet and went back into the sitting room, and lifted the pitcher in both hands, balancing herself by giving it her full attention as she carried it to the kitchen. "I'll dump the water out—you wouldn't want it to spill in your car—but do you want the forsythia?"

"Of course," Janet said. "It's so pretty—sometimes forsythia is kind of scrawny, you know? But this is just perfect."

So Estelle poured the water into the sink and handed the old green lemonade pitcher to Janet Northrup Keyes, who said, "Well, thank you again—I'll treasure this—"

"Enjoy the rest of your meeting," Estelle said, and opened the door and, at last, the woman was gone.

Estelle stood a moment with her back to the closed door. It was after five; dinner was at 5:30; she wanted to get her bed made, at least, before she went downstairs. She took a deep, deep breath and let it out slowly, and went into the living room and collected the cups.

The girl had bitten her fingernails so far there were scabs. She had whispered, and Mrs. LeTourneau had hissed, "Speak up." Mrs. Hennessey's hand had flinched, there on the shoulder of the girl's coat, but Mrs. Letourneau hadn't looked away from the girl. She had just folded her arms and said, "I'm waiting."

And what had the girl said? I'm very sorry I took this? Whatever she had managed, Estelle knew what her own reply had been: "I can't sell this now. You know that? It's no good to me." And the girl—oh, braver than Janet Northrup remembered herself being!—had glanced up with something like hope, rubbing the backs of her hands down her sides, and Estelle had met those odd golden eyes for a second before she picked up the little pin and dropped it into the trash can behind the counter. "I can't stand a thief," she had said. "Don't come in here alone again."

It was what she always said, what she had probably said sometime she didn't remember to the sweaty boy who had become the man in the bright shirt, and to a dozen others, not all of them Margaret Hennessey's, by a long shot. She'd been harsh, certainly, but stealing was wrong; they needed to learn that somewhere.

And lying was wrong.

She washed the cups now, and dried them, and put them into the cupboard, before she turned and considered the tulips. They glowed here now, in the dimness of the tiny kitchen.

She'd get her bed made up and then she'd go downstairs for her dinner, and take these and leave them in the dining room there, where, you never know, somebody might appreciate them. She touched the edge of one blossom. She might be able to find out what these were, and maybe plant some for herself. And she might find out where she could buy her own lilies. And you never know: once she got everything arranged the way she wanted it, she might invite one of the ladies from downstairs for dinner. For now, though, she'd been too many people today, and she was close to worn out.

~ ~ ~

The elevator bell dinged, and all five of them—Mr. Phillips was back again from wherever he went—turned to see the young woman step out carrying a handsome green pitcher of forsythia. She smiled, and Mr. Phillips said, "You'll want to get your gloves on—it's pretty nippy out there."

"Oh, it's terrible, isn't it!" she said, and she put the flowers down on the table beside the door and took a pair of gloves from her coat pocket and put them on as Mr. Phillips said, "Coldest March in eighteen years, they say," and Mrs. Coulter said, "I'm glad I don't have to go out in it," and then the young woman said, "Good night!" and went out.

"I thought you said tulips," Mrs. Linster said.

"Oh, I certainly said that," said Mrs. Crowley.

"Well, *that* was forsythia," Mrs. Coulter said. "Whatever she took up there, what she brought down was forsythia." She rapped her cane.

Denise came out of the office pulling her coat on. "Good night, folks," she said. "Enjoy your dinner—see you tomorrow," and she was gone, too.

Mrs. Richmond came down the ramp with her walker and went directly to the little case on the wall beside the elevator, as she did every night, and the others waited, as they did every night, and she said, "Ham and scalloped potatoes."

"Truth and beauty," Mrs. Crowley said. "All ye need to know."

Live Feed
Avra Wing

Our sons stream
from Chicago,
gigging,
guitar and drums,
at the Brown Rice
on Division.
We lie in bed
a time zone away
watching on a laptop.

Adult children,
oxymoron of loss.
They are there
and we are here,
and besides
what we spent
on music lessons
it has nothing to do
with us.

Free jazz means
they need to
sound each other out
feel when to join in
and when
to hold back.
To be
cohesive
and unexpected.

The set runs late,
but we stay
til the end
not wanting to miss
any of it,
though we can't
tell how it went
because the image
keeps freezing.

Find Something to Say

Avra Wing

I pick up the phone to tell my son
his friend's little brother
killed himself Tuesday
and here it is Thursday and I'll
make it short
because the lady who cleans
is waiting to vacuum.

I didn't know the boy, not really,
and didn't need to
to feel the weight of his life dropping through
Brooklyn, or the release of hearing
my son, in another city, answer.

He must speak to his friend.
I must go there, face the parents,
the brother. The grandparents.
Find something to say.

I will enter their empty, empty house
with the awkward sorrow
of an acquaintance, bringing
something picked up at the bakery
and dump it on the kitchen table
among rugelach and baked ziti
for people who will never want to eat again.
A cruelty even to suggest it.
But expected. We must do what is expected.

This child thought otherwise.

Signs and Wonders
Avra Wing

Today, on the way to school,
my daughter spots
a red helicopter
circling over Flatbush.
It's good luck, she says,
practicing augury on the fly.
Last week it was
a fortuitous seagull
a bit far afield
poised atop an SUV
on Seventh Avenue.

People once believed
birds signaled
what your odds were,
whether or not you had
a go-ahead from the gods.
I'm not sure my child,
at 12, knows this.
In her reading of the world
all these early sightings are
blessings on the day.
All signs point to yes.

The Man in the Old Calendar
Chigozie John Obioma

The footsteps of one man cannot create a stampede.
- An Igbo proverb

THE PORTRAIT OF the man in the old calendar was not the work of God but of man. The man is ashen-coloured and depleted in form. Raiment of rags flow down his waist like the portrait of Lazarus in dark skin. His face is blurred by excessive colour. Drops of the colour brown drag his ear a bit lower at one side; the colour black turns his face into the colour of an earthen statue. His teeth are like those of a savage confined to Neolithic caves. From the moment I saw this portrait, I knew at once that that it was not of him; this was a work of man, imperfect in every spectrum of life. This *man* sits at the centre of a calendar size 12 x 12 inches, covering a large portion of it. His hands are lifted in the same way as his face, towards the skies which above him are beautifully captured as a blue ripple in space stripped by near-invisible lines. Towards the top right-hand end of the calendar is the sun, shining brightly, with its phosphorescence splayed across the bluish horizon. Almost nothing showed it was him except for the writing that attracted me to the calendar as I was walking past that souvenir shop that morning. It read: *Abulu, the extraordinary preacher, seer and madman of Akure City.*

I knew at once, that I knew the man whose portrait they attempted to capture in the calendar. His name was indeed Abulu. He was a madman. Obembe, my elder brother, told me his brain dissolved into blood after a near-fatal accident that left him insane. His insanity came in two different realms as though two demons took turns in playing the accordion of madness in his head. It was the regular insanity that afflicted his mind most of the time, so that he merely played about naked, dirty, smelling, awash with filth, trailed by a sea of flies, dancing in the streets, picking up waste from bins and eating it, soliloquizing aloud, screaming at objects and all the things that stray derelicts did. At those times he walked about with his head forested with long colored hair, his face patched with boils and his skin greasy with dirt. He dangled his enormous manhood unabashedly like it was a million-buck engagement ring. He walked the city barefoot and almost mortally scarred his feet once when he unknowingly trod on a pool of shattered glasses when two cars collided on the road and their glasses were shattered to smithereens. He'd bled so much that he fainted and lay across the road beside the battered cars till the police came the following day and took him away with the cars. People thought he'd died. They were shocked to see him walk back to the truck six days later, his mutilated body covered in hospital clothes and his varicose-veined legs concealed in socks.

But there was something remarkable in him when he was in this realm of insanity and it was his independence. He didn't bother anyone.

Sometimes however, mostly in the evenings when the sun had begun to fade away, he would transform into Abulu the prophet. He would go about singing, clapping or preaching in a loud voice. He would go to people and tell them he knew what would happen to them in years to come. He would come into compounds with unlocked gates like a thief -if he had a prophecy for the people there. Sometimes it was said that even when he was in that realm of insanity and he came across people he needed to prophesize to, he would temporarily delve into the other realm and tell it to them. He would chase after a moving vehicle, for instance, crying out his prophecy if it was for someone in the car. Hence people sometimes turned violent when he tried to make them hear a prophecy. A woman once knocked him to the ground with the heel of her shoe. The swelling from the attack occupied a large area above his left eye and remained there. People feared him whenever he delved into that realm and they avoided him like he was a plague. It was said that his tongue harbored catastrophes. He was known to have predicted the ghastly motor accident that claimed a whole family. When Sola, the daughter of the man who owned the big cinema in the neighboring street died, it was said that she took her own life because Abulu had prophesized she would never marry.

~~~

When we were young, my brothers and I were fishermen. We used to trek the long tortuous path to the Ala River located at the outskirts of the city of Akure, a journey of twelve kilometers every day after school. The river was a myth in the village, it was believed to be a place where people dropped their murdered dead. Earlier that year, 1995, the mutilated body of a woman was found near the river. The city council would place a curfew on the river that would run from 6 p.m. to 6 a.m. We kept our trade secret for a long time so that the fishes and tadpoles lived and died inside the muddled waters in the old beverage cans which we hid in Ikenna's room. Then in May of 1995, nearly three months after we started fishing, one of our neighbors, a middle-aged woman who lived alone and survived by hawking fried groundnuts around the city, caught us near the river and told mother. Mother was furious; she seized our hook and sinkers and locked them up in the store behind the kitchen. When father visited us from his base in the faraway city of Yola that weekend, he made us lie down and gave each one of us grave whippings on our naked buttocks.

That was the last time we fished. From that night on, we began to hate the very idea of fishing. But oddly, father began to refer to us as fishermen. He made it a title which he added as a prefix to our names so that he sometimes called me fisherman Benjamin. But we soon began to hate that name too. Ikenna my eldest brother made us hate the name so much that when in 1997 a neighbor referred to us as *fishermen* while talking with mother, he suggested we punish the neighbor as a deterrent to others. That night, we climbed into her compound through the short fence and captured one of her chickens. We returned it to her doorstep, headless and dripping with enormous amounts of blood that trailed us all the way down to her house like a line of soldier ants. Although the woman never discovered the reason behind the mysterious slaying of her chicken, we were satisfied we'd gotten revenge.

But there were stronger reasons why we began to hate that name. A few days before the neighbor caught us near the stream, Ikenna had started trying to convince us to stop fishing. He'd pointed out many things that were bad about the stream that we never noticed before. He complained about how the bush around the stream was filled with excreta, that the fish were polluted, that he'd seen a sunken human skeleton underneath the stream, that Solomon was a bad influence and many other reasons. Even though the grave whippings on our buttocks bruised our passion to the bone, it was something else, an experience that killed it. It was an experience Ikenna and Boja had warned us to forget and never mention. They'd even made us vow never to talk about it and we'd promised that we would commit a lobotomy on our memories and disgorge every detail of it into bottomless pits. Yet Obembe and I talked about it when they weren't there. It was while Obembe was talking about it that mother got to know about it. True, it was that experience that killed the strongest passion we had and snatched every vein that flowed between Ikenna and the rest of us. That experience was our encounter with Abulu.

It was while we were returning from the river on an evening in May 1995 that we met Abulu along the sandy pathway a kilometer from the river. With an outburst of laughter, he drew our attention to where he was seated under some mango trees. We'd jeered at him and Kayode, the thin-armed boy who was then a year older than me at eleven, threw an unripe mango at him. Abulu caught the mango in the air and threw it high, so high like a javelin that we watched it descend in the distance far away. We'd clapped, called him a superman and turned to go when he called Ikenna's name.

"Ikena," he cried and we turned sharply, utterly bamboozled.

"Let's go on our way," Solomon suggested immediately. He pushed Ikenna forward onto the path. "It's not good to listen to Abulu's prophecies."

"No, he has something to say I guess." Ikenna wrenched himself free and moved away from Solomon as a small tear appeared on his Bahamas resort t-shirt.

"Ikena. Ikena." Abulu continued chanting Ikenna's name with a Yoruba accent that made it sound *Ikena*. When he had called it for perhaps the tenth time, he stopped. He rose from the ground to his feet and started again, facing us in the encroaching darkness.

"Ikena, your hands will become bound like a sparrow in the day you shall die." He put his hands on his eyes and demonstrated blindness. "You will be mute. You will be crippled."

He threw himself on the ground, knocked his knees together and fell backwards into the sand as though they'd been crippled and laid flat on the sand for a long time while we waited impatiently for him to continue. The sky had darkened now and the birds that nested around the stream turned into black objects that were not discernible to the eyes as they flew over our heads.

"Ikena, your heart will stop beating," Abulu continued aloud. But as he spoke, the burgeoning sound of an aircraft that was approaching from a direction to the east was intensifying. He cast a frenzied gaze up, sprang to his feet and continued in a louder voice that was whipped into faint whispers, like a sandstorm would blank out the sight of an emerald in the desert no matter its size.

Afterwards we all heard him say; "You shall die like a cock will die. You will lie fallow on the ground. *Ikena.*"

He picked up a handful of sand and threw it up. After the sediments settled, he turned to go, singing and clapping as he went.

Oh, father in heaven
I implore you to shred the firmaments to fulfill my words
I implore you to mutilate the seasons to give my words breath
Let none of them be lost.

When we got near home after the other children had dispersed, Obembe told us he'd heard everything Abulu had said.

"Then tell us what he said when the plane was flying past." Boja requested.

Obembe hesitated.

"Didn't you hear him?" Ikenna asked menacingly.

"He said that a fisherman will kill you Ike."

"What, a fisherman?" Boja asked aloud.

"Yes, a fisher. . .," he didn't complete it, he'd begun to tremble.

We walked on, bruised like we'd been beaten in a fight. We were almost at the gate when Ikenna turned to us and murmured that Abulu meant that one of us would kill him.

~~~

Obembe said Ikenna was never the same again after that encounter with Abulu. He'd believe at first that if anyone would fulfill Abulu's prophecy, it was going to be either Obembe or me. He then drew a long line between us and himself with Boja on his side. He developed hatred for us and spanked us constantly. We were neither allowed to go out with them nor play football with them. This went on for a long time. But as years went by, he began to draw another line where a dot had never been drawn before; a line between himself and Boja. Twice in 1998, they swore furiously at each other and would have fought had Lekan, Ikenna's friend, not stopped them. Next, Ikenna slapped Boja across the face over an argument and mother punished him. But they stopped talking to each other after that day and Boja descended like a fallen angel, a hundred light years from the edge and joined the rest of us.

The night Ikenna slapped Boja across the face, Obembe told me that Ikenna had become a python and was now living in trees above the rest of us, the lesser snakes. He would not eat ants like the rest of us. He completed his secondary school in May and got admission to study Electrical Engineering at the state university in July 1999, the month and year he turned eighteen. He began to boast habitually that he had become a man. Indeed, his head had shaped into the shape of a mango, like father's head and the boundaries of his mouth were beginning to flower with beard. Boja followed closely at sixteen. His beard had begun to grow too but was still too scant. Obembe was only fourteen, I was thirteen, David was six, and Rachael was four.

The next month was June, when mornings in Akure city fallowed with fog like manure. Boja woke up one morning from a nightmare in which hooded men fastened him to an altar and attempted to pluck out his eyes. His heart became swollen with anger. He'd stopped sleeping in the same room with Ikenna since February when Ikenna slapped him but he still had his things in the room. He would not move out, it was his room, his right. Whenever he needed new clothes, he waited until Ikenna woke up and opened the door. But that day, he did not wait for Ikenna to wake up; he went to the door after breakfast and began to knock. Mother had gone to the market with Rachael and David after breakfast. He knocked on but there was no response for a long time. Bulging with anger, he began to pound the door with his fist and cry aloud.

"Ikenna, open the door."

"Who is that madman that is disturbing my peace?" Ikenna thundered from within the room.

"Ikenna, you are the madman, not me." Boja replied. "You'd better open the door right now."

We heard a noise from within the room, then a pause, after which the door opened. Ikenna appeared and lunged forward at Boja.

"You call me a madman?" he cried, as his blow landed across Boja's face.

Boja crashed to the floor but immediately regained balance and knocked Ikenna backwards with his legs. Before Ikenna could rise again, he was back on his feet, swearing and cursing with a voice that frothed with fear and hate.

"I am ready for you today; I will give you that which you want from me. If this is what you want, come out to the open space so we won't destroy anything in the house." He dashed out through the kitchen door to the backyard where there was a space between the compound well and mother's tomato and corn garden. Boja closed the well with its metal lid and sat down on it, waiting. Ikenna came after him and they began to fight again, tearing at each other like gladiators. Obembe and I stood a distance from them, pleading that they stop until Ikenna knocked Boja to the ground again.

"If you don't keep out of this, I will give you both the beating of your lives," he cried. He moved towards us, his face forming into a fierce grimace.

With those words, he tied our hands like helpless cripples. We watched them fight on with a kind of vigor and intensity that was naturally uncharacteristic of boys of that age when they engage their siblings. Ikenna punched with a zeal that was far greater than he'd punched the chicken-selling boy at Isolo poultry market who called mother an *ashewo*, a prostitute, when she refused to buy his chicken during the yuletide season two years before. Boja kicked and lunged with more daring than he'd lunged at those boys who threatened to stop us from fishing at the river one Saturday morning. It was as though their hands were conditioned by a disposition they knew nothing of but that knew them very well, even to the littlest plasma of their blood. They fought in the sand, shredding their clothes, picking at each other's legs and crashing to the ground. Then, Ikenna slugged a blow at Boja's face and split his nose. Deep red blood gurgled down his mouth and dripped from his jaw to the ground. He sat there, weeping and dabbing his bloodied nose with the rags his shirt had become. We stood where we were, Obembe and I, pleading in a soft voice that they should stop. Ikenna stood over his younger brother, panting aloud and twisting his bloodied hands. He gazed up to the sky as though he had suddenly realized that it was Boja that was crouched below him bleeding profusely. He spat away and, cursing under his breath, he turned towards us. Just as he moved, Boja sprang up and lunged forward. In an unbelievable show of superiority in strength, Ikenna ducked and was on top of Boja again, punching wildly at his battered face. I could not stand it any longer. I told Obembe the best we could do was to get an older person to stop the fight. Flattened like a slate with fright, he nodded and we dashed off at once, our hearts pounding at the maddening rate of the blows that were raining down.

The man we found was Mr. Bode, the motor mechanic who lived just three blocks from our house. He'd just returned from his workshop to relieve himself at the latrine he shared with the other occupants of the bungalow he was living in. When we found him, he was washing his hands at the long-necked tap that sprouted out from the ground near the wall. We told him breathlessly what was going on in our house and he immediately turned off the tap and ran back with us barefooted. A long-bearded he-goat owned by our neighbors was sitting behind the gate in the midst of small black pods of its own feces, some squashed into brown, pus-like pastes, and others coagulated in twos and multiples. It was bleating with its tongue strapped out of its mouth like duct tape. Boja and I had beaten it thoroughly two days before. We were shocked as we passed by the dark-bodied and reeking animal, that the only sound we could hear from the compound was the *heh heh* sound of the goat's lousy breathing.

We took Mr. Bode to the backyard but there was no one there. There were just the bloodied rags and bloodstains on the ground. My brothers were not there. We were alarmed. In distress, we parted. I waded through the garden to see if they were behind it, probably hidden from us by the cornrows. Obembe and Mr. Bode went inside the house, calling their names as they went. Although I knew there would be no one in the garden, I reached the end of the garden near the brick fence before stopping to catch my breath. I heard in that moment, Obembe's loud voice, screaming aloud. I made a mad dash for the house and traced him to the kitchen. But he was not there alone. Mr. Bode was standing beside him, his two hands on his head, gnashing his teeth. But there was a third person who'd become a lesser being than the fishes and tadpoles and didn't even qualify to be called *a fisherman* anymore. His head lay facing the refrigerator; his wide-opened eyes were fixed in their place, seeing nothing. White foam pooled from the end of his mouth which was slightly closed, concealing a third of his dentition. His hands were thrown wide apart, one of them propped upwards as though he was asking for something he badly needed. At the centre of his stomach was the wooden end of mama's kitchen knife, its sharp blade buried in his flesh. When I saw this, I cried out his name and my tongue was lost to Abulu's so that the cry came out corrupted, slashed, subtracted from within, dead and vanishing. "*Ikena.*"

Ikenna was buried four days after his death, two days after father returned to us and the eve of the day we saw Boja again. Ikenna himself was perhaps the only one in the ceremony that was dressed differently—in white shirt and trouser—like an angel that had been caught unawares during a physical appearance on earth and had his bones collapsed to stop him from escaping back to heaven. Everyone else wore black clothing. The ceremony was almost concluded when Obembe began to cry and left me with the honor of being the only one who did not cry. Instead, my eyes were fixed on the vanishing face of Ikenna as the sand splattered on his head, his closed eyes, his nose, again onto his head and some fell down beside his ear in a bid to fill up the grave. I have now fully realized, like an awakening, that my brothers were all more than mere fishermen; they had different qualities.

Ikenna was a sparrow. Little things could unbridle his soul. Oftentimes, thoughts, slandering, wistful thoughts, combed his melancholic spirit in search of craters to be filled with sorrow. Once he sat at the corridor of the house, alone on a Christmas Eve while the others were in the house dancing and singing carols and eating cakes and drinking Cokes. As he sat pondering the impact of Aunty Anna's breasts and clean-shaven pubic area which he'd peeked at through the keyhole of the bathroom door on his penis and heartbeat, a bird fell down in front of him and didn't move. He made quietly towards it in the dark. When he was an inch from it, he dived towards it and his hands covered the feathery beast. It was a sparrow that was escaping from human captivity. A strand of rope was still wound round its leg. Ikenna guarded the bird jealously for three days, feeding it with whatever he could find. Mother asked to let it go but he refused. One morning he propped the bird's lifeless body in his hand. Heartbroken, he dug a hole at the backyard and buried the bird.

But Boja was fungus. He was fungus inside. His heart produced blood that was filled with fungus. His words were infected with fungus that had the capacity to inspire nose-splitting blows. His kidney was filled with fungus, so much that he didn't stop bedwetting until he was fourteen. Mother thought that he was under a spell—a bed-wetting spell—and took him with her for prayers. Boja was not just a fungus, he was a destructive fungus that could inhabit the body of a man, collapse his spirit, banish his soul and leave a mortal hole through which his blood would empty into the ground. He was also a self-destructive fungus. He needed no one to kill him; he killed himself and ate himself. He would not have floated on water if the fungus hadn't eaten him and caused him to decompose from the inside so that he began to float upwards in an upright position. He was found floating in the well in our backyard the day after Ikenna was buried. His photo, the one in which he crouched with his hand to the cameraman like he was going to knock him off the ground, was still popping up on the Ondo State television news commercials with the heading: *missing person*. The police were still frequenting our house to announce their slow progress in the search of him. We were having lunch in the sitting room when our neighbor, who had come to fetch water from our well at in the backyard, came screaming. She'd found his body floating upwards in the half-filled nine-foot deep well. We'd rushed out and found him, his hands lingering on top of the water, his clothes forming a parachute on the greasy water.

Obembe was a searchlight; the man who found the way, who discovered, who knew, who first saw things, who examined things and who when he was lost, would find himself. It was he who found out that there was a loaded pistol behind the sitting room shelf two years after we moved into the house. Father would take it to the police station, petrified but thankful it wasn't picked up by a younger child like David or Rachael. It was he who first noticed that Rachael was a polydactyl with twelve toes on her feet and twelve fingers on her hands and made mother cry and worry that it could be difficult for Rachael, her only daughter, to get a husband in the future with her condition. He'd noticed two days before we found Boja that the water he fetched from the well was greasy at the top and gave off a foul odor.

Obembe was also an omnivorous reader. His heart was omnivorous. It consumed in diversity and stored information as cuds which he regurgitated, chewed and spat them into my ears every night when we'd retired to our room to sleep. He told me many stories. The night Ikenna was covered with earth, he told me the story of Homer's *Odyssey*; he'd read a simplified and compressed version of it. The night Boja was dragged up from the well he told me the story of *Things Fall Apart*. I listened as usual in silence in the darkness that was mildly corrupted by the moonlight that settled in a long-drawn arc on the wall. His voice soared over the fan that was throttling in decibels against the distant gloom of the night's treacherous silence. When he finished the story, he sat on the bed and tapped me on the shoulder.

"You see, Ben, the white men would have been easily conquered had the tribe united and fought as one," he said with a broken voice. I sat against the wall to face him and our shadows crouched behind us.

"It's true," I said.

"Our brothers have left us today because there was a division between them."

"Yes," I muttered.

"Ben, do you know who caused that division between them?" I was puzzled, I tried to say something but my head felt empty. I hesitated.

"Do you know why Ike and Boja died?"

"No, " I resigned, breathing aloud.

He blew his nose into his shirt, and then he removed it and threw it on the floor. "Abulu." He said. "They died because of Abulu's prophecy. They died because Ikenna believed it and let it stay in his soul like a worm would stay in a living body. Abulu killed our brothers."

We sat in silence for a while, my memory drifting backwards and backwards until I was gripped with distress. Then I heard Obembe say: "I will avenge my brothers." He slugged his fist into the air and whispered: "I'll kill Abulu."

"What?" I was gobsmacked. "Why would you do that?"

Obembe stopped short of words. He gazed at me for a while. Then shaking his head he said in a defeated tone, "I will do it for my brothers, because they were father's fishermen too." He straightened out afterwards near the table by the window and next came the flash of two attempts to light his cigarette. Then he blew the smoke out of the window, sobbing noisily like a child.

~~~

In November, when the harmattan breeze turns people in Akure white as though they were mobile lepers who had to apply cans of Vaseline to their skins to fight dermatological graying, father opened a bookshop. A local carpenter constructed a large wooden signboard that was placed in front of the *Ikeboja Bookshop*. It was David alone who didn't know without having to ask that the name was a combination of Ikenna and Boja. Father told us he got 4,000 books for a start and that it would take him days to load them onto the shelves. On our way home, we saw Abulu coming out of a restaurant, a loaf of fresh bread propped under his armpit. He turned as we drove by and waved. Father drove past as though he didn't see him; mother hissed.

"Evil man," she murmured under her breath, "you will forever remain like this."

Obembe glared at me from the other side of the door where he sat. He had been avoiding me since the night I questioned his decision to kill

Abulu. Even though I was beginning to fear that he was drawing a line between us, the reaction of my parents and Obembe to the sight of Abulu that day mounted a nuke in my heart. It dawned on me that Abulu was indeed the cause of our common distress and the designer of our grief. It was he that planted that knife in Ikenna's stomach and threw Boja into the well. Abulu was our enemy. When we got home that evening, I told him I was ready to fight for our brothers.

For many nights we retired early to our room and switching off the light, we made plans on how to kill Abulu. We weaved a *coitus-interruptus* of imagined events and incidents, most of which we withdrew and discarded before they were fully formed. In turns, I saw us chase Abulu down the road on a windy evening and he fell into a running car which knocked him to the ground spilling the contents of his head on the tarred road. But Obembe said that the street people, those-ignorant-fools-who-don't-know-what-that-madman-has-done-to-our-family, will try to stop us. Next, Obembe imagined that we climbed atop the backyard fence with our catapults and waited for Abulu to pass so we could break his head with missiles. We thought about this one for a long time until I dozed off. When I woke up the following morning, Obembe told me that a few missiles wouldn't kill him off instantly and we could get caught too. Later that day, lying on our bed, we lay in wait for him at the Ala stream where he always went to wash himself in the evenings and followed him to the stream. As soon as he lay down to wash, we attacked him with our lines, Ikenna and Boja's lines too, perforating his flesh in multiple places with the hook until he died. It was Obembe who suggested this, and when he was done with it, he rose from the bed and lit a cigarette while I watched the shadow of his back on the wall.

For many days we went to the Ala stream with our lines and torchlight to guide us when it got dark, and waited for Abulu in vain. And twice, we flashed our torch on two naked men making love in the darkness of the shore. In one of those days, Abulu came and they chased him away from the river. We hid in the bush while they chased him and tried to catch up with Abulu after the men retreated but there was no trace of him. It was nine days before Christmas that we finally caught up with him alone by the river. On our way to the stream, we'd seen him chase a car, shouting in a loud voice.

"You will fall like a tree, Michael Oliga. Your children will . . ."

We waited by the roadside, the river was a kilometer away and we could smell the odor of dead leaves on its shores.

"Let's attack him." I whispered to Obembe when Abulu entered the path between the bushes.

"No," he said. "You can't be sure there's no one else coming behind us from the river or from the street."

We followed behind him until the river was close, then we hid in the bush and waited. The sun had set and darkness was gradually veiling the horizon. The spontaneous splash of water and singing from the river constantly struck the plexus of my heart so that it stopped beating for a while before picking up and starting off again. I waited cautiously for Obembe's command. Obembe first walked to the river slowly with pantomime motion to survey, and then returned and told me there was no one else near the river. Then he signaled that we rise, and we did. I couldn't tell why we cried out aloud as we lunged forward; it was perhaps because of the incredible rate at which my heart was beating and perhaps because Obembe had suddenly began to sob. Abulu was lying near the shore, facing the sky, clapping as he sang. We hammered the hook of our lines blindly at his chest, his face, his hands as he tried to protect himself, his legs as he tried to rise, perforating his flesh and tearing off chunks of it when the hooks stuck. We kept hitting, pulling, striking, shouting, crying, sobbing until the voices that had suddenly emerged behind us turned into the figure of two men, the men we'd flashed a week before. One of them held me from behind and wrestled me to the ground. I watched Obembe's shadow, running along the trees, calling my name out loud as the other chased after him. Immediately I sprang up and hit the man with the line so that he fell and I ran away as quickly as I could.

When we got back to our house, Mother was just returning from outside the gate where a mob had gathered, singing joyfully and tapping her feet on the floor in rhythm. Father was sleeping in his room but came to the sitting room when he heard the noise from the mob.

"What's the noise outside about?" he asked.

"There's a man there who claims he saw two boys kill Abulu near the Ala stream this evening and that the boys ran into one of the houses in the area when he chased them."

Father turned immediately to see if we were there. He found us both at the table, eating our plates of beans, absentmindedly.

I did not think the slobbering mouth of fear had left teeth marks on Obembe's back as it'd done mine until he poked the silence in the middle with a jab all of a sudden.

"Are you scared?" He asked.

He looked at me in the dark and shook his head.

"We'll go to prison if they find us," he whispered. "We have to leave this night."

"What, leave home?" I was astonished.

"Yes, right now."

He threw open the wardrobe and hurriedly began to pack clothes into his bag.

"Where will you go?" I asked.

"Anywhere." He'd started to sob. "They will find us by morning."

I watched him on until he zipped the bag. Then he turned to me and pointed at me.

"Won't you stand up from there now?"

"No."

He paused and sat on the edge of the bed. "They'll find us."

"Father will get us a lawyer, you shouldn't leave Obi."

He turned and pulled me to himself by my shirt. "If you won't come with me, then tell them," he cried. "Tell papa and mama that I...ran away."

For a long time Obembe sobbed against my shoulder. Afterwards, the window opened and the shadow of his body carrying a bag crouched like a gecko near the window.

"I will write you," he cried from the darkness.

I heard the thud of his feet on the ground just behind the window but I did not stand up to watch him go.

~~~

The next time I saw Father, he had grown a gray beard on both sides of his head. He could barely look at my face even though I sat between him and mama in the back of the car. Rather, his eyes scanned the streets as David drove us back to the house. I saw the old decrepit truck where Abulu used to live; a cockerel was standing on top of it. As we drove towards home, I asked him if Obembe ever wrote or came home these ten years that I'd been away.

'No, not even once,' he said contemplatively; he would repeat it three more times.

I was moved by what father had become—a morbid, lanky fellow whom life had bitten like a blacksmith into the shape of a sickle. He was still vibrant the last time I heard him say "fisherman" in the Akure high court, shortly before my trial. He'd told me to tell them all that happened and had reminded me again that I was raised to be menacing, a juggernaut and a courageous man. The words struck a constant refrain in my head as I went to the trial box. When it was my turn to speak, after the judge asked me to tell the court all that happened, how and why we killed Abulu, I'd first turned and gazed at him because I wanted to tell it the way he'd asked me to say it.

"We were fishermen." I'd begun.

But as my voice dashed into the stark silence of the courtroom, mother cried out and startled the court. I waited for the audience of the court to return back to me while father covered her mouth with his hand. Then when the judge asked me to go on with my story, I cleared my throat and started all over again so the words could come out refreshed.

"We were once fishermen; we used to trek the long... " I'd gone on and on, fearless, like father had wanted me to say it.

When we got home that evening, I stood outside our house and gazed at the street as if I'd just been born. So much had changed and I noticed a number of new big houses around. But my gaze was mainly on the road that sprouted into the distance. I was looking to see Obembe, the last of the fishermen. I had not heard from him in three months; I wanted to see him again, to tell him it was over. My fear was that he might not have received my letter. Yet my hope rested in the last words he'd written to me a month ago. *I will return the same day you return*. I leaned on this hope so that I remained in the sitting room late into the night when he came knocking.

~~~

Now, eleven years on, I see Abulu in an old calendar. I see the form of him that's passed beyond memory. Here in this portrait the structure of his life is still strong, edged like a stone pillar whose feet are solidly implanted in a granite pedestal. I told myself that this portrait was a remake of him, an attempt to come back into this world not by the hands of God but by the hands of man. But we'd sworn, Obembe and I, to destroy him—to wipe him out of the surface of the earth. With my hands quivering, my body hunched in the near darkness across from the heap of dirt in front of me which had sparked fire from the bottom, with the calendar squeaking as it burned up beyond all reckoning—I knew he would not return again. ▰

Head Games
Stephen Gibson

~ Rome train station

Catullus, nothing's changed around Termini.
In the bars, drunks roll off of counter
seats like roasted meats off of altars,
and whores lining the wall at the Twistee
ice-cream stand always promise me
every time I pass through here
to buy a train ticket to somewhere,
if they can't make me cum, it's free;
and the police (always in pairs) eyeball me,
but wait until I buy the ticket, then saunter
up to demand my passport. I stare
at my photo, nervous, because I'm guilty
of something, and any foreigner who can't tell
that by now hasn't traveled.

Details from Guido Reni's *Slaughter of the Innocents* (Vatican Museum)
Stephen Gibson

Unlike some war footage, this artist
doesn't turn away—one infant
is pinned, the sword all the way through
as the soldier looks behind him for release.
Who will gag the mother or tear off
her arms so that years from now

the soldier won't hear what he does now?
Who will plug the blackness the artist
has drawn for her mouth or tear off
her arms that wouldn't let go of her infant
that writhed like a bug in his hand for release?
Where does the soldier go after he is through

with this? What does he do through
the night to stop up his ears, which now
hear everything—and nothing? *Release
me*, the soldier's face seems to say. The artist
has the soldier look away from the infant
on his sword to the governor walking off,

whose back is turned, who's already off
to other matters because he's through
with this. For the governor, this infant
was an irritant he doesn't experience now
(the mother was something the artist
just didn't need to include). *Release*

*her from her pain—or don't; release
yourself from whatever, or don't—fuck off*,
that's what his back tells the artist.
Whatever else happens, he's through.
It's of no concern whatever to him now.
In the history of warfare, name one infant.

The governor turns his back forever. Infant
death in war is propaganda, a news release
from the side that's losing. It's like that now;
it will be in the future. The powerful are off
to other business. They are already through
with this. That's what his back says to the artist.

In one final foreshortening, the infant hangs off
of the sword, releases her hair, and reaches through
the plane as if the artist were now including us.

Crossing Sartre's Bridge with Inez and Estelle during the Iraq War

Stephen Gibson

~Venice, 2005

I found myself standing at the top of a bridge—
        really, little more than stone steps
arched over a narrow secondary canal—to watch

half a dozen gondolas and canal barge traffic
        get backed up. There was no exit.
There was nothing anyone could do. Nothing.

A small barge was jammed, sideways. Nothing
        the driver did could free it. From the bridge
you could see part of the problem: with no exit,

those behind pushed forward, though on the steps
        people shouted it was blocked, that traffic
couldn't go anywhere. On the wall, kids watched,

waved to their friends to come over. They watched—
        laughing, poking fun—because nothing
the guy did, like push against a hull the traffic

pushed into his barge, made a difference. On the bridge
        more people came to watch. The bridge's steps
filled with people, many shouting, others silent. It

was surreal. It made me think of Sartre's *No Exit*—
        people without eyelids forced to watch
but not understanding anything. On the steps

this one woman—there was really nothing
        special about her, she was on the bridge—
she just stood there and stared down at the traffic,

at this one gondola, wedged in by the traffic,
        being slowly pushed forward until it
bumped a boat stacked with Coca-Cola. On the bridge

the Italian woman waved to the gondola. I watched.
          An American woman shouted to her, nothing
that made sense, I'm sure, to the woman on the steps—

about seeing the Coliseum, the Spanish Steps,
          Trevi Fountain, the horrendous traffic
everywhere in Rome, the Vatican—but nothing

about Venice—and she was stuck in the middle of it.
          Not one word about Saint Marks. She watched
the woman above her nodding from the low bridge.

Coda:
On the BBC that night, I heard Bush talking: *necessary steps—exit
          strategy—Al-Qaeda—watch list—insurgents who traffic
in death.* I understood nothing. I was on that bridge.

Fur

Stephen Gibson

While we were waiting for the uptown express
on the 34ᵗʰ Street platform, this woman
came up to my wife, not threateningly, just
determinedly, as if she had something she
knew she had to do and was doing it
and my wife happened to be the object

of that single-mindedness, the object
being my wife's fur collar, whose express
purpose when her grandfather added it
decades ago was ornamental. This woman
was proving he was some tailor, though she,
of course, hadn't a clue—she was just

coming over to touch the collar, just
to take it between her fingers. I didn't object,
though she put me on my guard—she
wasn't threatening or anything, didn't express
some weird thoughts, didn't bark. The woman
saw the fur collar and wanted to touch it.

Something about the collar drew her to it,
so she touched it. She turned, smiled, just
like a little kid, the hand of this woman
stroking fur, then my wife, who didn't object
to a stranger touching her cheek or express
any kind of shock or fear, or anything. She

accepted the woman's touch. Maybe she
understood the woman's reason for doing it.
I didn't—whatever that woman needed to express
inside herself by coming up to a stranger just
to stroke a fur collar. Today, fur is an object
for rage, or worse. But not for this woman—

as my wife and I watched this woman
brush her fingertips along the collar, she
was as gentle touching the fur as if the object
of her affection could respond, as if it
were alive. The woman did this—twice—just
her fingers, back and forth, able to express

some need she just had to give in to this once.
And it was enough. Once the object was attained,
whatever need it expressed, the woman walked off.

Je veux te voir

Gina Barnard

I'm falling
              (I say to him)

into his eyelashes,
REM moving them
like caterpillars,
back and forth,

lashes touch-
squirm as lid-
skin breathes
the contractions
underneath.

Je veux te voir
I want to see you

does he remember
the dream he had
(underneath)?

Shorba
Gina Barnard

I usually wake up before he does,
open the blinds in the front room,
pause for a moment,
palm trees across
the street tousle in the breeze.

I walk back through the rooms, pick up
his water glass and bowl, take them
to the sink. Cracked wheat, chicken,
parsley, seven spices float in last night's
bowls. He made Shorba – Algerian soup
for the Ramadan meal to break his fast.

But this morning, he woke up before me
at 5am, packed one of everything.
I drove him to MEPs—
Military Entrance Processing Command.
Still dark—a line of future soldiers
about one hundred stood
in unmoving shadows.

What will they do?

I come home without him, still dark,
toss his wet towel in the laundry basket,
store his keys and sunglasses away.

On the kitchen counter, a half-eaten piece
of baklava left from the thirty
pieces his mother had sent from Algiers.

Waiting for a Call to Prayer

Gina Barnard

1. It is the month of Ramadan,
prayer times call out
on my computer.

4:09 it is *Asr*, afternoon.
The Muezzin's voice breaks through
silence, breaks through noise.

Vowel heavy—
as if to connote the world
of words singing in vowels.

Each stretch of throat,
a change in note.

Hayya ala salatt
Make haste towards prayer

Hayya ala el falah
Make haste towards welfare

2. You, not quite northeast now,
but east of me, nonetheless.

You have no time for
a moment's meditation.

Given new prayers,
the soldier's creed:

I stand ready
to deploy,
engage,
and destroy.

Boot Camp Discharge

Gina Barnard

I wait until it is late, dark
and quiet—daylight savings
turns us in early—as if
waiting in my spare,
familiar chair,
will bring you home quicker,
or the carrier, your letter.
You were promised
a role in diplomacy—an M16
fattening your shadow.
Other native Arabic, Farsi, Pashtu speakers
fell for the tricks, assumed this recruiter,
a brother, would not loot dreams,
or promise a bridge further away
from acceptance and survival.
You were on that ledge between worlds,
and now you're coming back for a revival.

Domestic Scene
Gina Barnard

Gunfire and the birds

down by the river
down by the river

we took a little walk
we took a little walk

aroma of lemon grass,
cilantro, broth

and watched them drown
and watched them drown

the little yellow bird—yellow
bird on the sill
wasn't safe
from his will

special forces
training demo
it's for people who want
to die. Yeah it's beautiful.

Is that your word?
No. They don't have beauty
in the army.

A yellow bird
with a yellow bill
came to my window sill
I lured him in with a piece of bread
and I smashed his little head.

Where are the lychees?
Hapapou,
Where are the lychees?

Gina Barnard

White hearts in syrup, white

hum of the old laptop heating up
heating up

the helicopter too low—
low

lychee in bowls, clink

ooh la la

is that the only phrase we know?
that's the only phrase.

There is a hardness inside its
heart-skin,
curled into itself.

I'm contaminated
I won't speak like an adult.

We took a little walk
aroma of broth
down by the river
and watched them drown.

The Beginning of Peace

Gina Barnard

A medium in Algiers reveals –
you are in love with a woman
from a village in the Kabylie Mountains –
Olives drop down my blouse
cool stone in summer
dusts my thighs
This is where I'm from –
A medium in Algiers reveals –

What You Would Give
Michael Copperman

"PASS ME ONE," my father says, and my younger brother Jeremy offers the Ziploc bag of sliced cantaloupe, the fruit fleshy and ripe. I hold the bag for trash. My father gnaws the melon to the rind, leaves no edible shred. He's never forgotten his childhood in Buffalo, he and his brothers fighting for the last scrap of meat. When he finishes he drops the rind into my bag.

We're at the beach, and the weather has cooled unexpectedly, coastal clouds pressing close, frothy breakers chopping in and receding weaker. Gusts of wind whip the surface to tiny peaks, fill the air with the brine of salt and drying seaweed. A sandstone cliff rises behind us, narrows into the vanishing line of sky and water and beach. We stand on the spit of sand amid the smoothed rocks, cracked shells and ribbons of kelp. My father and brother and I, eating fruit and watching the waves break.

When Jeremy's bag is empty and mine is heavy with discarded rinds, I place my bag in his and we set the whole thing at the head of the trail. Our shoes are there laid in a triangle, three pairs of tennis shoes and my father's knee-high sweat socks he also wears with sandals despite the way it makes my mother cringe. She's at home today, watching the Oregon football game on television with my brother's wife and six-month-old. That's how it is in my family: my mother follows football, and my father ventures into the wilderness for fifteen-mile jaunts, intent on getting his exercise. His resting pulse, he says, is fifty-five, an elite fitness level for a man of sixty. Today we hiked only four miles in, the shorter distance out of deference for my hip and ankle, though nobody would say as much. Now I'm limping, sharp streamers of pain running the length of my right leg, and trying hard to hide it. It will be a tough walk out.

Jeremy's in a good mood, joking and happy. He picks up a small stone, flips it at me playfully. I bat it away with my hand. When we were kids at the beach, we'd work for hours making sand castles, carving out moats and bridges and lopsided, tilting towers. When we were finished and the tide was encroaching, Jeremy would lose interest and race into the surf. I could never leave the castle, would linger bent double in the sand, frantically throwing up walls to stop the waves, to preserve what we had built, though the ocean always swept it away.

On the trail, Jeremy and my father talked of Rylan, of how at six months he can walk if you hold his hands, of how long he sleeps and why and when. My father is a family doctor, knows childhood development, and he told Jeremy proudly how far ahead of the curve Rylan was, how coordinated and strong despite having been a preemie. I was quiet because I had nothing to add, though I certainly think Rylan's a beautiful, strapping kid, healthy and gifted with a set of lungs that can break windows. When

I was nine months old, or so the story goes, my father woke to me howling in the night like I was being burned from the inside out. He immediately guessed what was wrong: a rare condition in infants called intussusceptions, where the intestine collapses on itself like a telescope and the entire system closes down. If not quickly diagnosed and dealt with through surgery, fatal septic rupture follows. My father shook my mother awake and the three of us sped to the ER, my father at the wheel with the pedal to the floor, my mother cradling me to her chest, not bothering with a baby seat with my siren-screams. At the ER my father informed the skeptical doc of what he suspected. The ER doc performed routine test after routine test. And though I can't imagine my father enraged now, the lines of his face worn to a permanent, benign composure, that night he yelled and pounded his fist on the examining table, swept papers from counters until the doctor agreed to do an x-ray. I was in surgery an hour later. Twenty minutes, another hour, and it would have been too late. My father saved my life.

About my nephew, I could have said, 'he's a handful,' and Jeremy would have nodded half-heartedly, because he knows I don't really understand. I hold Rylan when Jeremy and Erica visit, and I smile, make my own foolish baby sounds, but I don't take him by myself. The truth is, I'm terrified of not knowing how to calm him if he cries, if he needs something. What if he chokes on the formula? What if he has an emergency?

My father eyes the way I'm limping and grimacing. "That hip's not moving," he says. "It still hurt?"

I nod, and he steps nearer, eyeing my leg as if he can intuit what's wrong, then he shakes his head. "Got to get that insurance together, to go and see."

"I know, Dad," I say, and try to keep the peevishness from my voice. He's already examined me twice, has had to admit he has no idea what I've done. First I turned the ankle rushing to a class I was late to teach at the university. Then, I tried to keep running, and the way I adjusted to the sprain set off the hip. It is, in other words, something I've done to myself, and something he doesn't know how to fix. Like, I think, so much of what's come between us since I've grown beyond his ability to assess. We don't argue, and rarely have; an oldest son, I couldn't reject a legacy so substantial—my father is good, compassionate beyond reason, kind beyond tolerance. He works sixty hours a week when he could work forty because he insists on taking immaculate care of his patients, his bedside manner all quirky, ascetic saint: 'Have you pooped?' he can say without a hint of absurdity, impervious to normality. This also confers him the power to counsel a teenager about dope or deliver to the elderly the diagnosis of cancer not as death sentence, but natural next step. While I was growing up, he was infuriatingly patient, my childhood not a push-pull so much as a measuring, a striving to meet expectations set more by example than explanation. I came to understand life as a solitary struggle, for that was what my father had made for himself: the bike ride commute through the dawn, the affectionate distance from his clinic staff, who worshipped him but could recognize in him nothing of their own character. He touched no junk food, drank no beer or liquor, remained utterly devoted to my mother. Instead of taking drugs to combat the anxiety that kept him up nights, he worked out until his body yielded to fatigue, and when that failed, he meditated, achieved a calm he claimed was more restful than sleep. Sufficiency was located in discipline, the self capable of becoming so excellent an instrument of good that what you wanted selfishly or in weakness, you chose to forego.

For a long time, everyone thought I was perfect because I tried so hard and kept my cards so close to my chest. I was the high school wrestling star with the four-point who went away to Stanford on scholarship. My brother, battling from my shadow, was the one who needed to be bailed out of jail at three in the morning, the daredevil kid who skipped school to jump his bike from the roof to the pool or go surfing at the coast. My father was at a loss with Jeremy, and even when I was home from college he'd sit at dinner frowning, distracted, eyeing my brother tinkering with his bike through the kitchen window, Jeremy's head shaved clean and a metal stud glittering in his ear. I'd shake my head at his antics though I was doing my own hellraising away at college, pontificate gravely about his foolhardiness, how I hoped he'd mellow before the world hit back.

Even as a kid my brother was more generous with me. Once, play-fighting, I ran a sharp stick through his palm. "Don't tell," I pleaded, and because Jeremy knew how badly I feared getting in trouble, through his tears he nodded, and insisted all the way to the emergency room he'd fallen onto the branch. We were always two in crime, even in the tales my father spun putting us to bed in our dimmed room, sitting below me on my brother's bed, his voice muffled by the mattress between us, as if heard from a great distance. "Once upon a time," he would start, "there lived two boys named Michael and Jeremy, two brothers, together, in a city where it rained too much. They had a mother and a father and a dog named Suzy, but what they really had was a magic tunnel behind their dresser, a tunnel that led to a secret garden with chocolate covered cherry trees, rows of bubble-gum bushes and giant, rainbow-colored butterflies." In the stories, whenever my brother and I were punished (and we were somehow, always, both at fault) we would be sent to our room, where we would shoulder aside the dresser and crawl through the dark passage to the garden, where it was always summer and there was more candy than we could eat. Only on the edges of paradise did trouble lurk, in the dark forest with its spiders and snakes and worms. We would be called to action, and I would take the sword and him the bow and we'd journey into the wild, the two of us together invincible. In the end, we'd return to the garden and finally emerge through the magic tunnel in our room with our parents knocking at the door, checking to see if we were all right. The parents of the story never recognized their sons' secret heroism any more than my brother and I, listening to my father's voice in that place between waking and sleep, understood this to be his vision of our future, bright with inevitable success. My father would finish-- the brothers and family and garden all living happily ever after-- tuck the covers around Jeremy on the lower bunk and reach up and rest his hand on my leg for a moment before he left us to sleep.

The year Jeremy finished high school I pulled an all-nighter and drove nine straight hours up Interstate 5 to see him graduate. I arrived late, too late to meet up with my family, threw on a button-up in the parking lot and slid in the back, the only space left in the packed auditorium. When they called Jeremy's name and my father pushed him across the stage in a wheelchair, my brother gazing absently toward the ceiling, I felt things spin, and ran panicked for the rear exit, sprinted all the way around the auditorium until I found them, Jer staring with a distant glassy look, my father bent over him, wiping the line of drool trailing from the edge of his mouth. When my father saw the expression on my face he lurched back, gave me a harrowed smile that was meant to be reassuring, and said, "Don't worry, Mike. He'll be better in three weeks." When Jeremy's eyes focused finally on me, he formed a drugged, lopsided grin and said in a thick slur that was still unmistakably his own voice, "Mike, you're here."

The day before, Jeremy had driven my parent's van to the coast to surf with five of his friends. On the highway back that night, driving, warm finally after the cold Pacific and tired from a day of big, lovely breaks, he fell asleep at the wheel and drifted across the median into the other lane. They hit an older couple in a sedan head on at seventy, and everyone else except Jeremy was still in the hospital—his friends with broken legs, arms, wrists, some neck injuries, internal bleeding for Raitley, who'd been out of his seatbelt. The couple, with the smaller car and brittle old bones, had each sustained broken hips, the man a separated shoulder, the woman a shattered femur and cracked tibia. My brother, bruised blue up-close, with a severe gash on his leg and a sprained wrist, had gotten off the easiest. My father hadn't wanted to tell me during finals, thinking it would only distract me since there was nothing I could do to help. He hadn't considered my panic at seeing Jeremy and not knowing what had happened, not being sure, for a moment, what affliction had overcome him.

After that, my brother made gestures at being the kid he'd been. My father was right about his physical recovery: in three weeks he was walking without a limp, and soon enough he was taking long bike rides by himself on back roads, though I never again saw the ladder leaning on the roof. He went every day to the hospital to visit his friends and the couple, who were laid up for months. That September, he even tried going away to the surf-and-weed California college he'd been accepted to, but he couldn't manage to believe in anything careless. He came home after a year to the local university, got back together with his high school sweetheart, whom he married after college graduation. Then he started a catering business from scratch, bought a house near my parents' and a good-natured golden retriever, and when Erica got pregnant, he converted a room into a nursery with murals of trees and houses on the walls and glow-in-the-dark stars fixed to the ceiling. He made a home, a future, from his own trouble.

All the while, I was losing my idea of what I wanted. I'd finished graduate school and had no further predetermined path. My girlfriend Anna and I went under, which was my failure, my inability to commit to something I hadn't really planned. I know my father looks at me, alone since Anna left, and believes I should simply find the right girl, get married and have my own little Rylan. He does his best at restraint, but I know he misunderstands my silences, judges my occasionally caustic tongue, believes I go out too much. This morning, hiking, he pinched my belly grown slack from not being able to run on my bad leg and made some comment about beer guts and getting my cholesterol tested. He tells me I should be laying money away for retirement like my brother, suggests my job as an adjunct is below my potential, hints at how he'll help me with a down payment for a house the way he did Jeremy and Erica, once I 'finally' have a reason to buy one. He considers the way I live self-indulgent, and I don't know how to tell him it's not so easy, that I'm not him. That I'm trying.

"Dad, let's swim," my brother says. He's halfway to the ocean, pulling off his shirt as he goes. It's funny how he calls my father, now, to play—the kid who never needed his father for anything. My father looks at me. "Coming swimming?"

I look at the metal gray water, shot with white foam. The wind is cold. The water will be fifty degrees, icy and painful. I shake my head. "You go."

He nods, looks as if he wants to say something, then turns and starts for my brother, pulling off his shirt. He's still lean and muscular, his chest and shoulders shrunk from the memories of my childhood but still corded with muscle. Someday I will look like him, but I doubt I'll ever be caught skinny-dipping in the North Pacific in September. When he reaches my brother, who's already stripped naked, he pulls off his shorts and the two of them bellow, voices echoing off the cliffs, and race for the water, arms pistoning, white asses bouncing ridiculously, and throw themselves into a breaking wave, their heads and bodies gone for a moment before they surface, stand in the bubbling surf shoulder to shoulder, almost touching.

~~~

On the way home, my brother drives, and I give my father shotgun and sit behind them. By the time we made the car, sunset was past, and now it's full dark, the forest thick with shadows as it blurs past. My hip hurts now even sitting, a bone-deep ache that comes and goes. I was last in line going back so nobody could see my clenched jaw or my limp, but they still had to wait for me here and there, pretending to have stopped for water or food. Tomorrow the hip will be worse, but at least today I made it.

My father, more tired than he'd admit from the day's exertion, dozes in the reclined seat, his lips slightly open, snoring. Every few seconds he twitches, always a restless sleeper, troubled by his dreams, which are probably little different from his waking life: he no doubt strives to be perfect. I hope in his dreams he defeats his fears, though his worry runs so deep it seems unlikely. When he was twenty-two, his mother died of cancer, and whenever he speaks of the grandmother I never knew something in the pitch of his voice, the hesitation as he chooses his words, leads me to that quiet, dark-eyed young man, choosing medical school to find finally an explanation, a way to hold off death. His obsession with exercise and cholesterol and diet, with preventable risk, can be traced to that day. He contained his loss with only personal cost, only this unending quest to save every patient, and adequately advise his sons. When I think of my father, I am of the same opinion as his patients when they stop me on the street, having identified me from the photos in my father's clinic or the way I resemble him in the line of the jaw: "Dr. Copperman's a great man," they say, squeezing my hand or clapping me on the shoulder. "He changed my life." I agree, exchange pleasantries, don't mention I'm at a loss as to how he sustains his goodness. How from weakness he draws strength.

I can see my brother's profile as he drives, intent on the shifting lines of the road ahead. We pass a car in the other lane, and for a moment the headlights slash white through the car, light my brother's hard-set mouth and his hand tight on the wheel. He's tense. And then I realize: this is the highway, the same road and the same direction. Even the distance from town is about right.

I lean back in the seat, speak quietly. "You ok to drive, Jer?"

He blinks, keeps his eyes on the road. "Yeah. I'm fine."

I clear my throat. "Driven this road since—you know?"

He nods, leans toward the windshield as if to see better. "I have. But not at night."

My brother refused to see a counselor after the accident, refused to talk to anyone about it, even me. Still, in talking to my father about the facts, in imagining the time before the emergency response crew arrived and cut the van open, this is what I know: my brother woke moments after the crash, pinned through the leg by the seat chassis, which had been driven clear to the dash. The steering wheel had been pushed to his chest, bruising him with a barred circle like a peace sign. In the back of the van, his friends were screaming and whimpering with pain, pleading for help, and he could not move. He was held there for forty-five minutes in the dark, listening to them sob and cry, and knowing it was his fault.

"You know, I'd love to take a turn driving," I say quietly.

He gazes straight ahead for a moment, then glances at me and back to the road. I can see his hands in fists on the wheel, his knuckles white. "Ok," he says finally, and brakes until the car rests on the shoulder. The slowing wakes my father, who sits up suddenly in the front. "What's wrong?"

"Nothing, Dad," I say. "Just changing drivers."

He blinks the sleep out of his eyes, yawns. "Do you need me to drive?"

"I've got it," I say. My brother settles to the headrest for a moment, then he unbuckles the seatbelt and opens the door. I get out on my side of the car. The air is cool and sharp, the road black, without a headlight in sight. We're beyond the coastal cloud cover now, and above the jagged fence of trees the sky flickers with stars. The motor, which Jeremy has left running, chuffs and chuffs. I circle the back of the car gingerly, putting no weight on my leg. When I get to the driver's side I find Jeremy hasn't moved. He's standing, arms folded, staring up the dark road as if there's something to see. When I touch his arm he starts, shakes his head. "I don't know where it happened," he murmurs.

"The crash?" I say gently. My leg is shaking, and it will be awful trying to press the gas pedal. It's worse than I've ever felt it.

He nods, his face lit red by the running lights. "I looked for the place during the day, but I couldn't tell. It's no better at night. I can't remember."

I want to think of the right thing to say, but the throb of my leg punches red through my vision. I take my breath in sharply, let it out. "Why do you want to know?"

"I thought if I could find the place—" he stops, shakes his head. "I don't know, Mike. I don't know."

I grip his shoulder, squeeze and then don't stop because I'm steadying myself against him. "Neither do I," I say. "But I don't think the place makes a difference."

On the other side of the car, there's the sound of my father's door opening, then his voice, groggy and querulous: "You boys all right?"

I glance at Jeremy, who still looks a million miles away, and say quietly, "My leg hurts." He nods as if this makes sense. And he isn't thinking what I'm thinking, because he's back in that van with his friends begging for help he can't give, or he's driving again through the night wondering, was it right there? No, not here. There? He's gone where I can't though I would follow him through that tunnel if I could, locate the spot on the dark road, or lever him free from the wreckage so he can comfort his friends until the ambulances arrive. But there's no going with him. Instead, I'm imagining my father, a younger man, my brother's age or mine, shoulders broad and strong, startled from sleep by my scream and maybe not knowing exactly what was wrong, though his hunch turned out right. All he knew for sure was his son was in pain, and he would make it stop. Do whatever was in his power. And that night, it was enough.

"Come on," I whisper to my brother, taking him by the shoulders and pushing him toward the passenger side. Then I call to my father: "Dad, can you drive the rest of the way? Jer's tired, and my hip's killing me."

As Jeremy and I round the back, my father says something I can't make out over the engine noise, but I don't need the words to know he's agreed to drive, to do what we'll let him—anything at all to keep us from harm. ▪

The Unknown World
John Kay

I glue together pieces of
the pot she threw at the wall.

I pick up the pistol she left
and unload all but one bullet.

It had been holding down a poem
I had written while she slept.

I tie a pair of her nylons in a knot
and tuck them under her pillow.

The pigeons, long quiet, begin
to coo—when again, I welcome

her back from the unknown.
The bullet is for the demon.

After a poem by Mahmoud Darwish

Dead Man Walking
John Kay

He walks down the Bergstrasse,
sneering at the joggers, sure

that he's about to die—his
heart aching with every step.

He notices that all the yards
are brimming with red, white,

pink, and yellow rose bushes,
and before he can catch himself,

he's smelling one after another,
almost reviving. He keeps his

balance in the face of beauty—
which won't derail his destiny.

The Essentials of Western Civilization
Ed McClanahan

WAY OUT THERE at the far edge of the country, just off the campus
of Arbuckle State College of Education in Arbuckle, Oregon, that most
anonymous of towns, Assistant Professor of History Harrison B. Eastep,
MA, had once, in a previous existence, lived a largely anonymous life in
an anonymous apartment at an anonymous address, toiling by day deep
in the bowels of Lower Division Humanities at Arbuckle State (there was
no Upper Division), holing up at night in his apartment to grade papers
and drink blended whiskey and smoke dope and listen to his increasingly
unfashionable "progressive" jazz albums, while contemplating The Meaning
of It All. His second marriage had by now—let's say midwinter of 1967—
been dead almost three years, or about twice as long as it had lived. ("You
know what I think, Harry?" his wife, Joellen, had said tearfully on her way
out. "I think you're just *hiding* behind all that cheap cynicism! You're just
scared, Harry!" (*Cheap?* he'd asked himself when she and the boy were
gone. *If it's so fucking cheap, how come it's costing me so much?*) For the last
couple of years he'd been carrying on a half-hearted affair with a woman
named Marcella, a divorced librarian at the state university in Eugene,
forty miles away, but neither of them was enjoying it much (in large part
because Marcella's three teenage daughters persisted in treating Harry
like The Degenerate Who Came to Dinner), so Harry only saw her every
couple of weeks or so, when the sexual imperative asserted its insistent self.
Between times, blended whiskey (along with immense nightly cloudbanks
of marijuana smoke) provided all the solace he could handle.

Joellen had been right, actually: cynicism did come cheap in Arbuckle,
whose residents took great civic pride in the fact that they lived in the seat
of the only county west of the Continental Divide to support Alf Landon
for president in 1936.

Fort Leonard Wood, Missouri, where, as a clerk-typist in the U.S. Army,
Harry had spent two dismal years mindlessly typing recquisitions for laundry
soap and toilet paper, remains the only public facility in his experience that
could rival Arbuckle State for pure ugliness. The institution had begun life
as a teacher's college, but over the years its mission had gradually expanded
to include agriculture, engineering, home economics, nursing, accounting,
and a host of similarly romantic disciplines, with the result that the campus
itself was a preposterous confusion of uniformly unimaginative yet utterly
contradictory architectural styles.

The stateliest buildings were the ones that made up the original campus,
a cluster of eight or nine low, homely but serviceable crenellated red-brick
farewell salutes to the Industrial Revolution. They were closely surrounded
by several nice stands of elms and maples; in the spring the trees became

leafy ambuscades for great raucous flocks of grackles and grosbeaks that unloaded their sodden ballast only when Humanities faculty happened along the sidewalks below. One learned not to mind it much; in Oregon it was always raining something or other anyhow.

But looming over this bucolic litle patch of relative serenity was a farrago of towering slabs of steel and glass and concrete, thrusting themselves skyward as if to blot out the very sun itself (on those rare occasions when it endeavored to shine on this gloomy Joe Bltsplk of a campus), each of them—like the new Food Technology building, which the student newspaper proudly dubbed "the largest erection on the Arbuckle campus"—as impersonal and heartless as ... well, as the largest erection on the Arbuckle campus.

About the feet of these noble piles crept, kudzu-like, an impenetrable maze of interconnected one-story frame barracks, olive-drab relics of the Navy's wartime V-12 officer-training program. Here, in shabby oblivion, resided (or was bivouacked) Lower Division Humanities, including the Departments of Art, Languages and Literature, Social Studies, Band (not Music), and History, an Augean stable where Harry and his friend Gil Burgin shared a stall and plied their inglorious trade.

Humanities was a two-year "Service Division," ranking just above Maintenance and Janitorial. Its minions were regarded by the larger Arbuckle faculty much like the famous redheaded stepchild at the family reunion: Assistant Professors of Poultry Management looked down their beaks upon Western Civ instructors as if at indigestible insects; football coaches treated the poor devils who labored in the freshman composition line like something they'd stepped in by mistake. A distinguished Professor of Sanitary Engineering once openly referred in the faculty senate to required humanities courses as "a damned nuisance," and further denounced these la-te-da garnishments to a liberal education—in a soaring flight of rhetoric such as was rarely heard in that august chamber—as "frills, fluff, and frippery!" Students who evinced an unwholesome interest in the humanities were sent packing after their sophomore year, before the condition became contagious.

When Harry first came to Arbuckle, he'd supposed that he was under some personal or moral or even intellectual obligation to do his best to teach a little something, so he included an essay question in his first exam: he asked his students to discuss briefly some of the influences of the Great Plague of London on the religious climate of the time. The first paper he read began, "In this modren world of ours today, our modren medical science ... " The second paper began, "Daniel Webster, in his dictionary, defines 'influence' as ..." The third, "In his dictionary, Daniel Webster defines 'climate' as ..." Harry round-filed the whole batch of papers then and there and began immediately to make out another test, multiple-choice questions only ("The Great Plague was spread by: a. dirty doorknobs; b. old paper money; c. rats; d. illicit sexual intercourse"). Later, he discovered that true-false questions ("Sir Walter Raleigh caught the Great Plague from an Indian maiden in America and brought it home to London with him. T or F?") were even less bothersome to mark, and henceforward he relied on them to the exclusion of all other forms.

So it came to pass that over the years Harry's dedication to pedagogy eventually eroded to such an extent that when his mother first hinted, in a letter, that he might want to consider taking early retirement and coming home to Kentucky to go into the antiques business with her, he found himself, he confided to his officemate Gil Burgin, seriously entertaining the possibility.

"What?" cried Gil, as he scurried off to knock down yet another Western Civ section. "And give up the Life of the Mind?"

~~~

"HELL NO, WE WON'T GO!" shouts Assistant Professor Harrison B. Eastep, M.A., in unison with some two or three hundred youthful—and a few, like Harry, superannuated—resisters of the military draft, gathered on this sweet spring morn with their arms linked at the elbows to block the entrance to the Portland, Oregon, Induction Center, a four-story beige building of no architectural distinction whatsoever, ugliness excluded. It being Saturday, the induction center is closed, and no potential inductees are scheduled to arrive until Monday morning—a mere technicality, so far as both the demonstrators and their antagonists, a large, heavily armed contingent of the Portland police department, are concerned.

"HELL NO, WE WON'T GO! HELL NO, WE WON'T GO!"

Now let it be clearly understood that there is not the slightest possibility that Harry Eastep will ever be obliged to "go." After all, he's thirty-six years old, he's a father (albeit an absentee one), and he's already a veteran. (What would the troops at Fort Leonard Wood have done for toilet paper, were it not for the heroic efforts of Pfc. Eastep, bravely typing requisitions in the quartermaster's office?) No, Harry is putting his aging but still serviceable person on the line in solidarity with one of his favorite students at Arbuckle State, who has claimed conscientious-objector status and on whose behalf Harry has written several wonderfully artful letters of support to the student's local draft board, testifying to the deeply religious nature of the earnest young man's pacifist convictions, despite the fact that the young man in question is at best an agnostic, quite possibly a pagan, and most assuredly Professor Eastep's dope dealer.

Not to suggest, even for a moment, that Harry Eastep is any less staunch an opponent of the odious Vietnam war than the next right-thinking person. But up till now, his opposition has taken the form of appending his signature to supplicatory petitions and letters to the editor, participating in polite little on-campus peace marches, and bravely adorning his automobile with a bumper-sticker bearing the ubiquitous, iniquitous footprint of the American chicken. In other respects, however, he has made himself a bit more of a spectacle, having zealously taken up (being between marriages) certain other accoutrements of the Now Generation—such as long hair, a droopy moustache, bellbottoms, and granny glasses, not to mention all the sex, drugs, and rock 'n' roll he can stand. He opposes the war, of course, but he has been, let us say, distracted.

But there is something about the looming presence of a couple of hundred cops in the parking lot directly across the street—some astride great horses like Centurions, some bearing tear gas grenade-launchers, some with slavering, ravenous-looking dogs on leashes, the rest sporting huge coldcocks and flak vests and space helmets with spooky plastic masks— which, to borrow Dr. Johnson's well-used phrase, concentrates the mind wonderfully. The air in the no man's land between adversaries is poisonous with bullhorn commands, vile imprecations, tear gas. At this particular juncture, despite the defiant slogans and locked arms and revolutionary good intentions, Asst. Prof. Eastep has only one thought in his highly refined, pedagogical mind: how to get the fuck out of here unbusted, with his long-haired noggin unbludgeoned and his bell-bottomed lower person intact.

On Harry's immediate left is his friend and favorite student Freeman Jackson "Freejack" Harmon, recently defrocked Arbuckle State starting halfback (he and the coach didn't quite see eye to eye in regard to training rules), proprietor of an Afro so immense he could wear a peck basket for a fez, dealer in Acapulco Gold and other exotic enhancements to everyday human cognition. And right now, Freejack has Harry's intellectual-feeb left arm locked in the iron grip of Freejack's ex-halfback right arm to such an unrelenting extreme that there is not the slightest chance that Harry can escape without tearing his own arm off at the shoulder, like some small animal springing itself from a steel trap in tiny agony. Harry, in turn, has a nearly equivalent death grip on the left elbow of Gil Burgin, who is participating in this demonstration solely because Harry, as his friend and colleague and office mate, had appealed to his conscience (misery loving company, Harry had actually allowed himself to use that portentous word, though he did so with his own conscience as guilty as sin) and prevailed upon Gil (who also bought a little weed now and then from Freejack) to do his duty and join hands in expressing their unanimous, unswerving opposition to the draft and the war.

"HELL NO, WE WON'T GO! HELL NO, WE … "

Hell's rejoinder to this imprudent challenge arrives straight out of the luscious blue springtime Oregon heavens with a hollow *thwok!* on the pavement almost at Harry's feet, a hissing, spitting, fuming tear gas canister the size of a Colt .45 Malt Liquor can, hot as a two-dollar pistol, bouncing along in the gutter spewing hateful, noxious vapors. Freejack—who all morning has been wearing, mysteriously, a leather glove on his right hand—instantly turns loose of Harry's arm and reaches with his gloved hand for the canister as if noxious vapors were exactly what he'd been thirsting for, scoops up that scorching, virulent, vehement missive and in the same motion hurls it with all his considerable pacifist might straight back into the advancing ranks of the minions of the Dark Angel, looks back just long enough to holler "Scratch gravel, White Wind!" over his shoulder to his troops—both of them—, and takes off up the street through gathering clouds of tear gas. Harry and Gil exchange horrified glances, then break ranks and haul ass in hot pursuit.

After a few blocks Freejack swings down an alley and they catch up with him—which is to say, Freejack slows down, then stops and waits for them. When they arrive, breathless and staggering, ashen with terror, Freejack is exultant.

"You dudes!" he cries, laughing helplessly and slapping his knee. "Man, you the palest ofays in Portland!"

Gil Burgin is hugging a lamp post, gasping for breath. "Y'know," he wheezes, "Snakeshit had it right."

"How so?" Harry manages to inquire.

"Conscience," Gil says. "It really does make cowards of us all."

~~~

For all of Harry's carping and cavilling about his soul-destroying labours in the salt mines of Western Civilization, he eventually came to realize, over the years, that he'd somehow become rather good at the work. His classes were regularly over-subscribed, and in 1969, to his own astonishment and his department head's vast annoyance, his students voted him what the sponsoring student newspaper annually and invariably called "the coveted Teacher of the Year Award." Harry's department chairman at that time, a reactionary middle-aged young man who liked to be addressed, in correspondence and intramural communications, as Dr. Nelson R. Peckler, Head, denounced the award as a glorified popularity contest—true, but Coveted nonetheless, especially by Dr. Nelson R. Peckler, Head—and strongly hinted that Harry owed the accolade solely to his penchant for getting palsy-walsy with student lefties and acidheads and dope smokers— also true, perhaps, but quite irrelevant, considering that Nelson Peckler wouldn't willingly have allocated Harry a ten-dollar raise if he'd won the Nobel Prize for his tireless labors on behalf of the propagation of the Essentials of Western Civilization.

Harry and his pal-to-be Gil Burgin and Nelson R. Peckler, Ed.D., had joined the History Department of Lower Division Humanities of Arbuckle State College more or less simultaneously in the autumn of 1958. Gil bore an MA from Berkeley and a wife and two kids; Harry logged in with his measly MA from Ohio State, but was otherwise unencumbered; Nelson Peckler came loaded for bear, armed with that Ed.D. from some quasi-ephemeral institution in remotest Manitoba along with an overweening Sasquatch of a wife and four (and counting) toothy little Pecklers who would just as soon bite you as look at you. Harry and Gil entered as Instructors, "Dr." Peckler (he would not have appreciated the quotation marks) as an Associate Professor on the fast track for advancement. In 1962, in lock-step accordance with incomprehensible department policy at the time—four years up or out—, Gil and Harry, having committed no sins quite egregious enough to get themselves fired, both made assistant prof, and were granted perpetual tenure and simultaneously assured that, as regarded rank, they had reached the apex of their careers at Arbuckle State, and might want to consider some other line of work. Peckler, in the meantime, had already made full professor and was scrabbling up the ladder to Headship, a distinction which he was destined to achieve within a few more years.

Harry had liked Gil, his new officemate, right away. A lanky, handsome young hipster with a chiselled Dick Tracy profile, astonishingly black eyebrows, and a fast lip, Gil was double smart, he read books, he played piano with an ad hoc campus jazz combo, he voted left, he had even smoked a little weed in grad school (as had Harry, a time or two, in Columbus's murky mid-1950s dens of Bohemian iniquity). Because they both liked to come into the office at night, when the place was abandoned and quiet, to grade papers and work up the next day's classroom blather, they logged a lot of hours in each other's company. Gil and his wife, Marge, took pity on Harry, during his periodic (and ultimately chronic) bachelorhood, and regularly invited him to dinner, so that he became an intimate of their household, and a sort of de facto uncle to their kids, for whose innocent delight he recited the poems and riddles and tongue-twisters ("Sherman Schott and Noah Knott shot it out. Knott was shot and Schott was not, so it was better to be Schott than Knott … ") that his granddaddy had taught him on the front porch swing at the homeplace down in Kentucky all those years ago.

And Gil and Harry had another bond: a mutual, overarching loathing for their colleague and boss-in-waiting Nelson Peckler, coupled with that eminence's reciprocal contempt for the two of them. Peckler—"Nelson R. Pecklerhead," as the two young wags had taken to calling him, between themselves, years before he'd actually scaled those Olympian heights—was a large, soft-bodied, wide-rumped one-time third-string football player for a third-rate state college somewhere in Missouri, an individual scant of hair and intellect and principle but hungry, withal, for power of the more petty varieties, the power to schedule Saturday morning eight o'clocks for insubordinate subordinates, the power to impose his mossback politics on curriculum and textbook selection, the power to pat and pinch department secretaries (observed) and the occasional student cutie (rumored) whenever he could get away with it. ("Peckler the Inspector," the secretaries called him, or, alternatively, "the Handy Man.") Despite his vaunted Ed.D., he knew but little history, and his classroom lectures were reputed to be crashingly dull—much as he lusted after it, he would never win the Coveted Teacher of the Year Award—, nor was he popular among his colleagues, who were regularly galled by his ambition. But these deficiencies did not at all impede his rise, for, as a former third-string jock, he was an ardent fan of Arbuckle State's athletic teams, the Beavers, and those Beavers who signed up for his classes (they were legion) found Professor Peckler to be, in their case at any rate, exceedingly generous in the matter of grades, a fact which did not escape the notice of the grateful, sports-happy Arbuckle State administration—especially that of the president, an unreconstructed old warthog named August L. Shitemeister—and which went far to make the professor's ascendancy through the ranks both swift and sure. In 1968, a scant ten years after he arrived on campus, he was enthroned, and so became, in very truth, Dr. Nelson R. Peckler, Head.

It was never in the cards that Gil and Harry would become fast friends with Nelson Peckler. In the first place, their own educations had taught them, if nothing else, that even a puny Master of the Arts could trounce a Doctorate in Education any old time—that, indeed, the "Ed.D." appended to Peckler's name branded him not as a learned man but rather as something of an ignoramus. Unfortunately, they weren't as successful as they might've been at keeping their estimation of him to themselves: their first fall term at ASC was barely underway when Gil, during a departmental committee meeting, openly corrected Peckler's grammar ("That was actually a kindness," Gil told Harry afterward. "If he'd said 'the reason is because' one more time, I would've had to shoot him.") And later, at the annual Homecoming Day Alumni Barbecue, at which new faculty were expected to dish up lunch for the alums, Peckler made bold to take charge of the operation and imperiously order Harry to don a paper apron and cap and hand out Dixie Cups of ice cream at the dessert table, whereupon our hero did—in very truth—suggest that Dr. Peckler go take a shit in the ocean. Thus was their enmity sealed early on, and forevermore.

Over the ensuing six or seven years, as Nelson Peckler marched inexorably toward dominion, Harry and Gil engaged in many small skirmishes against him, and actually won their share of tiny victories; for despite the rising Peckler influence within the department, change was coming just as inexorably to the college as a whole:

Way back in 1961, the pacifist son of the Beaver track coach, of all people, had strode onto the football field during an ROTC halftime Homecoming Day parade bearing a sign declaring, before countless thousands of non-plussed Beaver football fans, "MILITARY EDUCATION IS NOT EDUCATION FOR DEMOCRACY!" President Shitemeister endeavored to expel the renegade transgressor, but failed, thanks to a petition signed by a heavy majority of his faculty and vigorously circulated within the history department by Gil and Harry, over the violent objections of the president's new protege, Professor-in-Waiting Peckler, who branded them (plagiarizing his own hero, the late junior senator from Wisconsin) "handmaidens of the Communist conspiracy."

It developed that the young pacifist had fired the first shot of a revolution that would mightily shake the Arbuckle State campus, as similar incidents would soon be shaking campuses everywhere. In 1963, the faculty dress code—coats and ties at all times in the classroom—came tumbling down. (That didn't do much for Gil, who continued to look ultra-cool in those skinny suits and ties of the era; but Harry immediately took up jeans and sweatshirts and, eventually, bellbottoms and frootboots and paisley-printed big-sleeve pirate shirts. Gil had the history department's first beard, Harry its first ponytail. Needless to say, Nelson R. Peckler was mortally offended.)

In 1964, a Young Turk professor in the English Department ventured to teach Vladimir Nabokov's dangerous novel *Lolita*, and the maiden lady who served as Dean of Students sent a student spy with a tape recorder into his class; the tape recorder was discovered, and the incident became a scandal that brought down Arbuckle State's entire system of *in loco parentis* rules, and allowed boys and girls to cohabit in the dorms, and girls to stay out until two or three or four o'clock in the morning if they chose to do so. Then came the resistance to the Vietnam war, and teach-ins and sit-ins and be-ins, and even, in Harry's case, between marriages, the occasional love-in; again needless to say, Nelson R. Peckler ... did not participate.

There was even talk that Arbuckle State College might someday soon—once it had disencumbered itself of the current administration of August L. Shitemeister—finally declare itself a genuine University, and offer degrees—even *advanced* degrees!—in those formerly despised fields known contemptuously as Lower Division Humanities.

~~~

In the final days of 1967, Arbuckle State College's venerable president August L. Shitemeister was gathered at last unto his fathers, but not before, as one of his final official acts, he had assured the elevation of his pet professor to the exalted position of head—or, rather, Head—of the History Department. Later that same academic year, Arbuckle State University did absolutely become a reality, and began to expand its offerings accordingly. Among the new programs was a Department of American Studies, which outraged the highly refined sensibilities of the History Department's distinguished Dr. Pecklerhead by incorporating in its curriculum, along with all manner of other licentious—possibly subversive—childish infatuations, the study of such low-life musical diversions as Nee-gro blues and jazz, as well as folk and soul and hillbilly trash and even that incomprehensible, unsavory new phenomenon, rock 'n' roll.

Now it happened that Harry Eastep, notoriously tuneless and tone-deaf though he certainly was, knew a little something—more than a little—about those very subjects, as well as about other arcane areas of the American Studies curriculum, including motion pictures and popular culture and literature, and especially about the work of his personal literary hero, Erskine Caldwell, in Harry's opinion the most overlooked, underrated writer in America.

(Except for rock 'n' roll, a late arrival which synthesized its predecessors, all these enthusiasms had come to Harry way back home in Needmore,

Kentucky in the bloom of his youth. He had, for instance, fallen hard for "race" music when he was fifteen, the very first time he heard, on late-night radio out of Nashville, a stirring tune called "Work With Me Annie"; had learned to love Hank Williams on the Craycraft's Billiards jukebox while shooting nine-ball with his pal Monk McHorning; had become enamored of the movies while popping popcorn at the New Artistic Theatre; and had come to admire the sublime work of Erskine Caldwell while standing by the revolving paperback rack in Conklin's Drugstore, surreptitiously reading *God's Little Acre*.)

Over the eons that Harry had been affiliated with what had become, for him, the Department of the Essentials of Western Civilization, he had been contributing essays and articles about all those subjects to obscure academic journals of American folklore and popular culture. But the pre-Peckler department chairman, a doddering old gent named Dr. Summerset, himself a Shitemeister-annointed wartpiglet, would have regarded such publications as Communist-inspired incursions on Western Civilization, so Harry hadn't even bothered to report his little successes to his nominal superiors, figuring they would probably count against him anyhow.

Nonetheless, his efforts hadn't gone for naught in the grander scheme of things, for it happened that the up-and-coming chair of the new American Studies department, young Dr. Toddler, had been reading Harry's work for years—had in fact cited and quoted from it liberally in his doctoral dissertation at Brown—, and was amazed to discover, when he arrived at Arbuckle State, that this Fount of All Knowledge was ignominiously slaving away in the bowels of what had until recently been Lower Division Humanities, teaching four sections of Western Civ. He summoned Harry to his office and offered him a proposition: Dr. Toddler aspired to publish, under the aegis of his spanking new department, a quarterly—*The Northwest Journal of Popular Culture*—, and he hoped that the eminent Assistant Professor Eastep could be persuaded to become its editor. He proposed a shared teaching position with Harry's department: half-time in the trenches of Western Civ, half-time at play in the editorial fields of the Lord.

The fly in this delightful ointment was in the person (so to speak) of a very large insect of the genus Peckler, who would have to sign off on the whole scheme, and was hardly likely to be cooperative. Last spring, when Harry and Gil and Freejack had been under seige in that Portland daisy chain, they'd been featured the next morning in a large photograph on the front page of the Sunday paper, *The Oregonian*—the three of them arm-in-arm, Gil in his usual sharp black suit and narrow tie, Harry long-haired

and bell-bottomed and tie-dyed to a fare-thee-well, and Freejack, with his
prodigious Afro, like a giant black dandelion—, above the caption "ASU
PROFS, EX-JOCK DEFY DRAFT!" On Monday morning, bright and
early, Peckler callled Gil and Harry on the carpet and charged them with
bringing disapprobation and contumely upon all of Western Civilization,
or at any rate upon the Essentials thereof, and sternly reminded them that,
henceforward, their every move was under the intense scrutiny of … The
Head!

At the time, the threat didn't mean all that much to Harry—his tenure
protected him from getting fired, and he was already condemned to eternal
Saturday morning eight o'clocks anyhow—, but it presented a major
problem for Gil, who, during the years while Harry had been writing paeans
to his rustic idols in the quarterlies, had striven mightily to earn a Ph.D.
at the *real* state university, forty miles down the road. Gil had finally taken
his degree, with distinction, just weeks after that infamous episode at the
Induction Center; and with the expanding curriculum, he hoped that he
might fall heir to the occasional advanced class, maybe even a promotion.
But der Peckler had proved unforgiving, and now, with a new academic year
well underway, Gil was still an Assistant Prof, still doing, perforce, his usual
four sections of involuntary servitude while he grimly plotted his appeal to
the faculty grievance committee.

So of course when the American Studies proposal came along, Harry
knew immediately that he too had a problem. He explained the difficulty to
his new best friend Dr. Toddler, who was sympathetic, and readily granted
Harry a few weeks to come up with a strategy. Later, Gil and Harry had
talked their situations over at great length, and gloomily concluded that
the grievance committee—which was, unpropitiously, Peckler-appointed,
and therefore under his pernicious thumb—might have to be their only
recourse.

~~~

On a Sunday afternoon a couple of weeks later, Freejack dropped by
Harry's apartment to see if he was interested—and he was, he was—in a
lid of newly arrived Maui Wowie. The transaction completed, they tasted
and, like the song says, got wasted; and eventually, during the rather aimless
conversation that ensued after they regained the power of speech, Freejack
mentioned, a propos of nothing in particular, that Harry's boss—here
Freejack was unable to suppress a marijuana giggle at what he was about to
say—Harry's boss must be one hip dude.

"Peckler?" Harry scoffed. "A hip dude? C'mon, man!"

No lie, Freejack assured him, explaining, with many more giggles of the same description, that a certain chick of his acquaintance who sometimes babysat the wee Pecklers, and who called herself Rainbow (Harry knew Rainbow from his affinity group at a teach-in a year or so ago, when she was still Mary Lou Suggins) was telling her closest campus friends (among them Freejack and a select few of his associates whom Rainbow sometimes condescended to ball) that Dr. Peckler, while driving her home night before last after a baby-sitting gig, having somehow discovered that she occasionally modelled for life-drawing classes, confessed his own long-suppressed artistic yearnings, and offered her forty dollars to let him take her picture, topless, with his new Polaroid.

And when Harry declared that he didn't believe a word of it, Freejack showed him what he claimed were the very same two twenty dollar bills that Dr. Pecklerhead had paid Rainbow for the Polaroids he had taken of her in his office yesterday afternoon—an away-game Saturday afternoon, when the campus was basically shut down—, the very same two twenty-dollar bills that Rainbow had, in turn, paid Freejack not two hours ago for a lid of the very same most excellent weed that Harry himself had just purchased and, indeed, the very same weed that he and Harry had, with such exceedingly satisfactory results, just smoked.

"Twenty bucks a titty, dad!" Freejack added happily, slapping his knee. "Rainbow's cool, she could care less. And"—he stuffed Peckler's pair of twenties back into his pocket—"the bread was right."

As soon as Freejack left to continue his rounds, Harry twisted up, for meditative purposes, a fresh doob, torched it, and sat back to think the whole thing over. There had to be a way—he told himself, as his fading high magically bloomed once again inside his head, and with it his resurgent hopes for becoming the exalted editor of *The Northwest Journal of Popular Culture*—there had to be a way to turn this information to advantage.

Peckler wouldn't dream of taking such pictures home, Harry reasoned, not with that great beetle-browed brute of a wife looming over him; so if said pix existed at all, they would reside somewhere in Peckler's office. This circumstance was actually quite heartening, in light of the fact that he and Gil, during their midnight explorations of the premises, had been surreptitiously invading that forbidden sanctuary off and on for years, having discovered long ago where Mrs. Sowersby, the department secretary, stashed the key, in a little niche in the top drawer of her desk in the front office.

The first time they went in, during the reign of old Dr. Summerset, Peckler's predecessor in the chairmanship, they were looking for the personnel files, for the purpose of ferreting out any unfavorable disclosures about themselves. (Gil's were clean, but Harry found a letter of "recommendation" from one of his former history professors at Ohio State deriding as "Freudian trash" a term paper in which Harry had propounded the theory that the impetus of the Westward Movement was rooted in the famous twinned myths of *penis captivus* and *vagina dentata.* Harry instantly pulled the letter from his file and tore it to bits, and boldly dumped the pieces in Dr. Summerset's own wastebasket.) Later, they'd gone in several times to get a look at forthcoming departmental exams, with an eye to preparing their students accordingly. More recently, after Peckler's ascension, they'd gone so far as to poke around inside his very desk on a fishing expedition, but had found nothing more damning than a stack of three-by-five cards bearing really dumb dirty limericks ("There was a young man from Corvallis/Who had a very large phallus ... ") in Peckler's own hand, suggesting—though not proving—authorship. The discovery was nonetheless an eye-opener, in light of Inspector Peckler's massive venting about moral decline on the campus during the *Lolita* scandal. But hypocrisy isn't an actionable offense, not even in academe—especially not in academe—, so in the end they were obliged to let it pass.

The trick, then, would be not so much in getting their hands on the evidence, as in how to take advantage of it. For a brief, delicious moment, Harry envisioned another headline in the Sunday *Oregonian,* something like PECKLERHEAD EXPOSED BY UNDERLINGS! TITTIES TELL TALE! But that wouldn't advance either Gil's promotion or Harry's own editorial aspirations, and anyhow he knew that neither of them had the stomach for that sort of direct assault on their persecutor. Nor was out-and-out blackmail an option; sweet as it would be to have the upper hand at last, Harry really couldn't imagine either himself or his almost equally mild-mannered colleague making that hoarse, hankie-muffled, midnight phone call: *"Okay Peckler, play ball—or else!"* Despite their readiness to sneak like, yes, burglars into Inspector Peckler's private office and pry into his very own personal effects and private art collection, there wasn't a criminal bone— well, hardly a criminal bone—in their liberal pinko bodies. Still, a few tittie pix might go a long way, a very long way indeed, toward righting certain wrongs against the underclass ...

Next morning in the office, Harry regaled Gil with Freejack's toothsome tale, to their mutual delight. But they both understood that nothing at all could happen till they had successfully verified that the pictures did, in fact, exist—and they agreed (almost without even saying so) that they'd best not let the grass grow under their feet: that very night, it was written, they would once again invade the realm of the Prince of Darkness, and see what they could see.

~~~

Having blown—thus far—two short-lived marriages with nothing to show for them except his lost baby boy and an enthusiasm for good eats (fostered by the fact that both wives had been excellent cooks), Harry had, of necessity, taught himself the rudiments of culinary art. Accordingly, in preparation for the evening's huggermuggery, he fortified himself with a bacon-wrapped filet mignon, a baked potato, and three generous glasses— call it a bottle—of an exceptionally nice little red, a favorite of Gil's from his own Napa Valley hometown. Then, anticipating a small late-night celebration in the event of a successful conclusion to their larcenous work, Harry stashed a second bottle of the Napa Valley red and a substantial fat-boy of Freejack's finest in his briefcase, along with a draft of the essay he was currently working on—"Criminality, Judgement, and Redemption in the Delta: Howlin' Blind Muddy Slim and the Epistemology of Despair," for *Backbeat Quarterly: A Journal of Undiscovered American Genius*—and, around nine, betook himself back to the office for their date with destiny.

Gil was already there, diligently poring over the weekly essay exams that he alone, of all his Western Civ colleagues (certainly including his friend Harry), still resolutely inflicted upon his students—and, of necessity, upon himself as well. Both he and Harry knew what was coming, and felt no need to talk about it; Harry planted himself before his Olivetti and began pecking away at his own essay, glad that, at any rate, he wouldn't have to submit it to Gil for a grade.

They fretted away at their separate chores, more or less in silence, till almost midnight, when Mr. Dingus, the night watchman, came through the building on his final round. As was his habit, Mr. Dingus stopped in their doorway to make his usual remarks about still burning the old midnight oil, eh?, and about the weather—damp, of course—, and to remind them to be sure and lock up after themselves, now, and then trekked off into the night.

"Welp," said Gil resolutely, when the back door had slammed shut behind Mr. Dingus, "it's gumshoe time, old son."

Together, Gil and Harry made their way down the dimly lighted hallway—each of them manfully resisting the impulse to tiptoe even though they both knew perfectly well that there wasn't another soul anywhere in the building—and let themselves into the front office. Gil went to the mimeograph machine and began copying tomorrow's pop quiz—a ruse, in the highly improbable event that they would have to explain what they were doing there in the first place—, while Harry invaded Mrs. Sowersby's desk and extracted the key to Fort Peckler, as per the groundrules they'd adopted during many a clandestine midnight foray into the enemy's redoubt. Then, with the mimeograph machine clattering away, Harry opened Peckler's door just wide enough to let Gil slip inside the darkened office and close the venetian blinds.

That accomplished, Harry hit the light switch, the flourescent overheads flickered, and suddenly the room was flooded with light, featuring Peckler's desk as though a spotlight blazed down upon it. Grinning conspiratorially, Gil and Harry briefly pantomimed the old Alphonse-Gaston routine, and then Harry, after the approved fashion of spies, cat burglars, and similar snakes in the grass since time immemorial, did the honors, sliding the shallow drawer all the way out to reveal, in the furthermost lefthand corner, the stack of three-by-five cards bearing, on the top card, Peckler's latest contribution to the collective poesy of Western Civilization ("There was an old man from Eugene/Whose penis could scarcely be seen …"), and, underneath that, another little stack of …

Polaroids! Yes! Tittie pix galore, eight of 'em in all, the entire product of what was, for the primordial Polaroid cameras of the day, a whole roll of film, eight fetching little black-and-white shots of the amply endowed Rainbow with her peasant blouse gathered down around her waist and wearing, from there up, only an insuppressible smirk—not unlike the well-known Mona Lisa smile, although perhaps rather more condescending towards the artist—that graced each and every photo.

"Ho-lee shit!" Gil and Harry murmured, almost in unison, when the photos were all spread before them on the desktop.

Despite her youth, Rainbow proved, in the titty department, somewhat droopy. But that had hardly discouraged her avid portraitist, who featured the celebrated appendages in every picture, usually at the expense of the top of poor Rainbow's head, which, like a mad scientist in a two-bit horror movie, he had lopped off quite indiscriminately. And best of all, every single one of the photos showed, in full view on the wall just over Rainbow's naked left shoulder, the tiny but perfectly legible image, as good as a signature on each and every masterpiece, of the framed diploma of Nelson R. Peckler, Ed.D.!

"So," Harry wondered aloud, after a long moment of silence while he and Gil stroked their chins in deepest cogitation, "what next?"

"Okay," Gil said, finally, "here it is: You take one, and I'll take one, and we'll put the rest back just like they were."

Harry was aghast. First thing tomorrow morning, he protested, Peckler, being Peckler, would no doubt sneak a peek at his new treasures, and would know right away who …

"Exactly," said Gil. "Just so."

Now Harry got his drift: of *course* Peckler would know that his two bitterest enemies, who were on the premises almost nightly, were the prime—indeed, the only—suspects, but what could he do about it? He was not without a blustering, bullying sort of courage, but, like Dickens's Mr. Bounderby, he could see as far into a grindstone as the next man, and he'd soon realize that, given his situation (PECKLERHEAD EXPOSED!), discretion was his only refuge. His goose was cooked, his ass was grass, they had him by the shorthairs; they could forget the heavy-breathing midnight phone calls.

Harry and Gil exchanged quick grins and muffled chortles (which spoke volumes as to their estimation of the Peckler intellect), then Gil grabbed two photos while Harry scooped up the remaining six and tucked them neatly back into their nook in Peckler's desk. They turned off the lights, re-opened the blinds, locked the door, replaced the key in Mrs. Sowersby's desk, gathered up Gil's quizzes from the mimeograph machine, and beat it back to their own office, where they collapsed into their respective desk chairs in paroxysms of mirth and self-congratulation.

After they had more or less regained their composure, they turned the two photos titties-down and shuffled them on Gil's desk, blindly selected one apiece, and filed them in manila folders in their respective file cabinets, under "T." That done, Harry went to his briefcase and brought out the celebratory bottle while Gil produced the corkscrew from his desk drawer (they had a long-established celebration ritual, usually reserved for the end of a grading period), and they each dumped out the paperclips from the innocent-looking café glasses on their desks and poured themselves two brimming slugs of the nice little red.

(The two Polaroids, by the way, are destined to repose on file until the following spring, when Peckler, to the surprise and delight of all of Western Civilization—or at any rate of the Department thereof—, will announce that he is resigning to accept a position as Superintendent of Public Schools of Fungo County, Alabama—and Gil and Harry, hearing the news, will gleefully tear the little pix to shreds and festoon each other with tittie-pic confetti.)

So there they were, just raising their glasses to toast the success of their midnight mission, when there came a soft tap-tap-tapping at their office window. His heart in his throat, Harry spun in his chair, expecting to see, at best, Mr. Dingus, and, at worst, Peckler, the Dean, the entire campus police force, and the House Un-American Activities Committee all assembled on the lawn outside the window like an out-of-season band of malevolent Christmas carolers … and beheld instead just one dark face, grinning maniacally.

Freejack.

As Harry, giddy with relief, rose to go to the back door to let him in, Gil put his finger to his lips in the traditional mum's-the-word gesture, to which Harry acceded with a nod. By the time Harry returned with Freejack in tow a couple of minutes later, Gil had found a clean coffee cup and was pouring their guest a welcoming dram of the nice little red.

Freejack shook the raindrops out of his Afro and sat down, meanwhile explaining that he'd been walking across the campus after a party somewhere, and had seen their light on, and thought he'd come in out of the rain for a minute. Harry, remembering his manners, dipped into the briefcase again and came up with the fattie, fired it up, and passed it over to him.

"Thanks, Teach," Freejack said, taking his hit and passing the smoldering doob on to Gil. "So what's happenin'? Looks like you dogs havin' a little party your ownselves."

"Ah, yes," said Gil, ready as usual with the exit line: "'Tis a naughty night to swim in."

Then, noting that Freejack looked more than a little puzzled, Gil took his toke, winked at Harry, and added an attribution: "Snakeshit."

~~~

But any proper academic treatise (which this chronicle certainly aspires to be) ought to have a few footnotes. So …

The following morning Dr. Nelson R. Peckler, Head, showed up bright and early, entered the front office whistling merrily, picked up his mail, gave the long-suffering Mrs. Sowersby an affectionate—albeit unwelcome— squeeze, and softly closed the door of his sanctuary after him, securing it with a click of the inner lock. After ten or fifteen minutes (according to later reports from the other secretaries), the door burst open and he stepped out, glowered about him as though, like his own flesh-eating children, he were looking for someone to bite, then turned on his heel and went back in and slammed the door. He stayed closeted, out of sight, until he knew that Gil's and Harry's eight o'clocks were over, then came storming out again and stomped down the hall toward their office, steam fairly issuing from his ears. He arrived at their door glaring ferociously, and found both miscreants seated at their desks, dutifully taking care of business.

Harry and Gil, having individually run through, overnight, numerous mental rehearsals in preparation for this moment, put on the most disarming smiles they could muster, and blithely bade him good morning. Peckler, venomous toad that he was, puffed himself up and opened his mouth to spew forth what would surely have been an unprecedented volume of invective, opprobrium, and calumny … and then, almost visibly, thought better of it, brought himself up short, snapped his great mouth shut again, swallowed hard, and slowly deflated to his normal cumbrous proportions. The jig, he had seen as plainly as though the terrible fact were lit by lightning, was indisputably up.

"Morning, fellas," he said at last, in honeyed tones accompanied by a smarmy leer that put their own disingenuous smiles to shame. "You fellas have yourselves a lovely day, now."

And with that, he slunk off down the hall and, for all practical purposes, out of the picture for good and all.

The following week's edition of the inter-departmental newsletter announced that Assistant Professor Gilbert Burgin, Ph.D., had been promoted to Associate, with all the perquisites attendant thereto (next term, though of course he doesn't know this yet, Freejack will be enrolling in Associate Professor Burgin's new upper-division "Literature as History" seminar, where he will inadvertently get some Snakeshit on him, and decide to become a writer), and also that Assistant Professor Harrison B. Eastep, M.A., had been appointed editor-in-chief of the new *Northwest Journal of Popular Culture*.

Neither of them was ever assigned another eight o'clock.

The Roar the Day After

Anne Haines

You love the way it makes your ears feel:
the world is just a little muffled, just
a little farther away. You know it was
the lead guitar that did it, scorched
its way upside your head until this morning,
nine hours later, you still feel it
throbbing like a tooth, like a body
of water. You wear your new black
tour t-shirt like a badge, throwing peace
signs to the other black tour t-shirt
kids between classes. It was something
real, the show last night, something bigger
than you know how to name. The stage
was the center of the universe and the man
at the microphone was holding something
you wanted suddenly, wanted so hard. Not
his beautiful guitar, though you'd give anything just to lay your hand against
its strings, to lift its slender neck heavenward;
not the pick he slipped into your outstretched hand
like a stealthy love note, though it made you
feel like Michelangelo. You love
the residual bruises of thunderous
applause and how bits of lyrics
come to you all day swollen with fever
and meaning. But mostly it's the echo
in your ears, how it makes you feel—
as you stumble through the hallways, as
you drum your pencil against the metal
of your desk, as you sketch guitars in the margins
of your notebook while the teacher talks—
like you're safe inside a private
room, one for which the admission
is the price of one more show, one more
encore, waving lighters in the air
until the whole arena spun and glittered.
It's that light that gets inside you
now, roaring in your ears. You'd rather
buy records than beer, rather catch
a ride to a show the next town over

than take the prettiest girl to any dance.
You'd rather feel the muscle of the drums,
the roar of where you think this might
be going, the way it makes your ears
ring like a promise, like a mission, like a vow.

Carne: Five Ways
Melissa Scholes Young

THERE ARE MORE than fifty different words for *carne* (meat) in Portuguese. Not surprising for a meat-addicted country, but shocking to a vegetarian moving to Brazil at the ripe age of 23. My husband, Joe, and I are newly married and we have chosen South America for a few years to teach and to travel. The new marriage isn't my concern; the new teaching jobs don't worry me; the unknown travel seems exciting; but being vegetarian in a country famous for *churrascaria* (barbecue) terrifies me. My nightmares wake me and I have to grip at my stomach, clawing at the perceived invasion. I learn two basic phrases in hopes of protecting myself: *eu sou vegetariana* (I am vegetarian) and *não come carne* (I don't eat meat).

~~~

1. Feijoada
Selma writes the recipe down for me on a napkin. The napkin is bleached white, and her handwriting is loopy like a lovesick teenager. She writes in green ink and draws hearts around her name. Selma is older than my mother. At our school she is *Dona* Selma, everyone's aunt, the matriarch of the Portuguese program, the biggest gossiper on campus. When Selma walks across our campus, students flock to her calling out *Dona*; they melt into her fleshy bosom and smile when she kisses them on their cheeks. Selma's many gold bracelets chime in the wind and the clicks from her high heels precede her. When *Dona* Selma arrives, the waters part.

Selma and I sit poolside at our principal's house listening to Samba. The music ringing in my ears is too loud. Selma drains her third *caipirinha*, Brazil's national drink made of crushed lemon, sugar, and *cachaça* (sugar cane brandy). I sip my first and feel lightheaded. She says the *caipirinhas* are to be served as an *apertif* to *feijoada* and I wonder if she'll invite the other Brazilians over to laugh and point at me if I pull out my pocket dictionary. I understand about every three words. I am lost in the rest of her language. I lean back in my plastic chair, woozy, content, and watch drunken Americans try to dance. They look like children, waving their hands in the air out of rhythm. They spill their drinks. They smoke cigars. They stumble and fall and try to catch each other.

> *Feijoada*—Dona Selma's recipe
> 2 kg. black beans
> 4 *paios* (Portuguese sausage)
> 4 *linguiças* (Italian sausage)
> 2 kg. *coxao duro* (fresh meat)
> ½ kg. *cebola, alho, sal* (onion, garlic, salt)

"Eu sou vegetariana," I say. Selma nods her head in agreement. "Sim, muito vegetais!" she tells me. Yes, you can add many vegetables. I try again but Selma just keeps smiling and agreeing. "Não come carne," I declare. "Não carne." Selma's smile disappears. She leans forward, pats my knee—the gold from her bracelets bangs against my flesh—and points to the dance floor. "Go join your friends," she says in perfect English.

~~~

2. Piranha Fishing

They sound like a typewriter's keys clicking in mid-air. Click. Click. Click. Go the piranha's teeth as it bites away at a stick. Our guide, an Amazonian native with a machete tucked into his shorts, pulls the piranha off my fishing pole and holds the stick in the fish's mouth to demonstrate. I am twelve inches away from the piranha's clicking in a canoe with three other strangers, *touristas* all of us, on the Amazon River. The piranha is only six inches long, with shiny, silver gills, but its mouth opens as large as its body. The water is brown and muddy; it reminds me of the Mississippi I grew up on. The water is choppy and strewn with trash; gasoline oil pools in bubbles on the surface. Our canoe wanders into a dense, weeded area and the tall grasses brush my knee. The sound from the bugs is deafening. Joe is in the canoe behind us, I think. The men in our group have been separated from the women. I'm afraid to turn around, to look for Joe and threaten my balance on the plywood bench. We are seated single file, wearing blue ponchos with the name of our tour group stamped on our backs in white lettering: *Tours de Amazonia*.

I seem to be a natural at piranha fishing. I'm a little disgusted with myself, but I have decided that even a peace-loving vegetarian like me needs to fish for piranha in the Amazon. No one will know but Joe and me. When in Rome and all. At least that's what I tell myself. Every time I lift my bamboo pole from the water our guide grabs the line in mid-air with his bare hands and pulls off my piranha. He smiles at me like a proud father. He tosses it into the bucket between his legs. The piranhas protest and beat their bodies against the plastic hard. I want to look into the bucket, I can almost see them if I lean forward, but I'm afraid. Piranhas gasping for water, biting each other bloody. I think it must be some justifiable punishment for their carnivorous nature. I feel superior. I deny all hypocrisy.

When the bucket is full, we canoe up to a dock with a small open-air shelter. A woman and a man grab the bows of our canoes and tie us to the side of the dock. The woman is wearing a dirty apron smeared with blood.

They help us onto the land, hand us bottles of water, and motion to the benches where we are to wait. The piranha bucket is hoisted over the side. The woman strains under the weight and disappears into a makeshift kitchen. The children, barefoot and almost naked, run around us, swiping at rocks and sand with their sticks. They smile and wave at us. They laugh and gently push each other toward us, daring the other to get closer. They are beautiful. I can't stop taking their pictures. We are called to the shelter, seated ceremoniously at a table set with dishes and linens, and the man and the woman stand beside our table watching, waiting. "Muitos obrigados," I say, offering my thanks and returning their smile. "Não come carne." The woman nods, "Sim. Sim." Yes, yes, we understand. The man ladles out soup into our bowls for lunch, and just as I lift the broth to my mouth, the piranha head—teeth, skeleton, eye balls—floats to the top of the bowl. "Delicioso," I say, pretending to slurp my catch.

~~~

3. Rosario

What I will remember most about this night is the corn ice cream. Kernels of ripe yellow corn swimming in vanilla bean. The kernels burst in my teeth as I try to smile convincingly. "Mmm. Interesting," I murmur. *Muito interessante*, I try. I am standing in the marbled foyer of our new headmaster's *Lago Sul* home. This is the wealthy part of our city, where the foreign nationals buy houses. This is our official welcoming party for all the new American teachers, twelve of us all altogether. Veteran teachers mingle with the Brazilian staff of our school. They move in and out of Portuguese and English easily. The house is a mini-mansion to me and I've counted five maids and three butlers since we arrived. Everyone ignores the servants, and I can't get used to it. It's as if we are all supposed to pretend they aren't there, swirling around us filling our drinks, offering us food, cleaning up our spills. We are all middle-class Americans, displaced to this country to teach middle-class American children whose parents have displaced them, too. We don't have maids in our country. But in Brazil we can afford as many as we want. Maids to cook for us, to do our laundry, to clean, to watch our children. Joyce, the school's Brazilian secretary and my favorite so far, drains her beer and leans into me. She watches me watch the maids. "You want maid? I know good maid. I'll send you maid tomorrow."

And she does. The next morning I hear a knock and a buzz from our apartment door. When I open the door, Rosario waves and says "Joyce." She has a round face and black hair pulled into a bun. She's wearing a dress of cheap cotton that doesn't fit. The buttons look like they are about to pop and free the rest of Rosario. She smiles broadly and I see four or five teeth. I like her instantly. She doesn't speak a word of English. I don't yet speak much Portuguese. I lead her into the kitchen and show her the maid's quarters, a tiled room off the back of the apartment. She waves me out of the kitchen. I sit alone in the living room, pretending to read a book. Rosario moves among the rooms picking up laundry. She starts the washing machine, runs soapy water in the sink for dishes. She comes back to me and motions her hands to her mouth repeatedly. I realize she is asking if I'm hungry. I think I hear the words for rice and beans. She stands before me waiting. We stare at each other. Rosario walks her fingers in the air. Ah! I get it. She's saying she'll go shopping for groceries. "Sim, sim," I nod. Yes. "Eu sou vegetariana. Não come carne." Rosario stands there smiling. Oh! She's waiting for money. I pull out some Monopoly money from my purse—the bills are red, blue, and green with faces I don't know—and hand it all to her. Rosario takes one bill, shakes her head at me, and stuffs the rest back in my purse. She rambles in Portuguese an entire paragraph. I don't understand most words, but I definitely hear *carne*. "Eu sou vegetariana. Não come carne," I repeat. She waves her hand bye-bye and I return to my book.

A few hours later I awake from a nap and hear Joe and Rosario talking in the kitchen. I join them and I am quickly rushed into my first Portuguese lesson. Rosario is pointing to things and saying their names in Portuguese. She laughs every time we try to pronounce them, too. Finally, Rosario points to the clock on the wall. It's time for her to go. I get my purse again and hand it to her. She shakes her head, takes out another bill, and nods. When she leaves, Joe and I inspect the piles of clean clothes, the sparkling surfaces that reek of bleach, the pots of food still warm on the stove. I sniff the food suspiciously. When I open the oven, I find a huge hunk of meat boiling away in a shallow pan of onions, carrots, and potatoes. Rosario has ironed every piece of clothing we own, including my husband's boxer shorts. She's put pleats down the front of Joe's underwear. A full day's work for the equivalent of twelve American dollars. We look around our house, which feels empty now without Rosario, and we have nothing left to do. We package up Rosario's food and deliver it to the guards of our apartment, huddled in their tiny booth at the bottom of our building. They turn off the miniature black and white television when they see us coming, potholders in hand, pans of offerings, the smell announces us and they smile.

And so it goes for the next two years. Every Tuesday Rosario appears, scrubs our apartment, takes money out of my purse, and leaves behind a boiling pan of *carne*. We try to explain our vegetarian diet. When our

Portuguese fails, we write her a note. She pretends to read it and nods *Sim, Sim*. We are worlds apart. Joe and I are educated middle-class Americans with the luxury to choose a vegetarian diet for moral and ethical reasons. Rosario is from a satellite city of Brasilia. She rides the bus two hours each way every day into the city to clean and cook for Americans. Her world is poverty where anyone who can afford to eat meat would never refuse the luxury. To Rosario, vegetarian equals poor and we aren't poor.

Our guards begin looking forward to our Tuesday visits and food offerings. When we return from work on Tuesdays, they greet us more enthusiastically and pat their stomachs when we walk by. They fall a little in love with Rosario. I suspect it's all a conspiracy.

~~~

4. Tofu Hunting

One afternoon I am in search of tofu for dinner, surprisingly easy to come by in this meat-loving country. Because of the local immigrant Japanese population, which flocked to Brazil in the early twentieth century, there is an abundance of sushi and tofu in Brasilia. They pack the rice with strawberries, apples, and mango. I've been going to the local Asian grocer and buying my tofu in yellow blocks in bags of water from the refrigerator, homemade. The woman behind the counter is a delightful enigma. Her face is Japanese, but she speaks Portuguese. She is second-generation Brazilian, and every time I visit the store, I expect something different, something not like Portuguese, to come out of her mouth. I've heard that a sushi restaurant in our neighborhood makes tofu fresh daily, so I decide to try to buy it there and save myself the three block walk to the Asian grocer.

I find the restaurant easily and wait by the counter studying the takeout menu. A young Brazilian woman dressed in a Japanese robe greets me. With hand gestures I explain that I am only here to buy tofu. She tells me I have to go to the back of the restaurant and buy it from the kitchen, but then she stops me when I try to walk past her. *Não*, she says, *Saida. Saida.* I know that means exit, but I don't understand why she's telling me to leave. She takes the menu from my hand and draws a circular arrow. *Saida! Cozinha!* I back out of the restaurant, holding my menu and her arrow map. Standing on the corner, facing the restaurant, I see an alley leading to the back of the kitchen. I point to it and the woman yells, *Sim. Sim. Cozinha!* The alley leads me to the back door, where I knock and wait. An old Japanese woman comes to the door, drying her hands on a towel. The brown wrinkles around her eyes make her look like she is squinting. She smiles when she sees me.

Soja? Tofu. I ask and hold out my bag and money. *Quanto?* she asks. How many? I show her two fingers and she ducks back inside the kitchen. When she returns, she holds the bags in her hand and takes my money. I reach for the tofu, but she pats my wrist.

"Não," she stops me and shakes her finger at me. "Fala que prepara," she commands. Tell me how you'll cook this.

"Que?" What?

"Quiero saber voce prepara soja." I want to know how you cook tofu.

"Eu no sei." I don't know. It's my answer for everything.

"Ah! Primero…" She begins explaining how I will cook her tofu.

She refuses to hand over the tofu until I agree to her cooking method. She makes me promise to drain and press the tofu before I fry it. I mimic with my hands her instructions. I hold my pretend frying pan in the air and show her when I'll turn the tofu. She takes me into the kitchen and shows me which oils to use, which oils to avoid. I nod my head in agreement. She speaks rapidly in Portuguese, I understand little, but I mumble "Sim" every time she pauses. Then she presses a packet of spices into my hand and holds up her finger to her mouth. "Shh!" She winks at our secret exchange. Then she hugs me, kisses me on both cheeks, and puts the tofu in my bag.

~~~

5. *Rodizio* Service

In my nightmares, this is what I see: uniformed men with sticks of meat waving them under my nose, their long silver skewers smoking with barbequed flesh, maroon-colored sauce dripping onto my shirt as the waiters descend on me, and I am saturated in the earthy smell of *carne*. On my first visit to a *churrascaria*, this is what I see: men with sticks of meat and large knives, bearing sharp, white teeth in smiles, begging to carve me a slice of flesh. My meat-loving parents are visiting Joe and me for the first time in Brazil. Their one request is to eat at an authentic Brazilian *churrascaria*. My father has done all the research. The guidebooks proclaim this one to be the best. I love my parents, I'm giddy at their visit and willingly pay the one hundred *reais* bill per person (about fifty U.S. dollars each), and I'm trying not to gag at their request.

My parents are hard-working Midwesterners. They own and operate a family pest control business. They raised my brothers and me on ten acres of land in rural Missouri where we grew pigs and chickens and a garden so big it yielded most of our food for the year. My father got a chicken ready for dinner by putting his neck between two nails on a tree stump and cutting the head clean off. Eyes wide-open, the tiny beaked head fell to the ground. The chicken ran headless to the pond and lay down on the bank polluting our swimming hole with their blood. My mother plucked and boiled and fried. Dad bragged that no one could clean a chicken like my mom. The bird body was smooth and creamy with puckered dimples where the feathers were once attached.

I am a vegetarian by marriage. It was practically in my wedding vows. To have and to hold and to not consume animals or their byproducts. I said yes. Joe has been a vegetarian his entire life. He doesn't know how to eat meat and his body probably wouldn't tolerate it well. His parents once lived on a hippie commune and learned to farm organically. They are militant and all natural and my conversion to their way of eating was a welcome relief. Joe's parents would never set foot in this *churrascaria*.

But Joe and I have set out on this South American adventure alone, to determine our own way, to see what we become. Where and who we are from is always prominent in our thoughts, but we've come here to experience other ways of being, to learn to navigate this world on our own, even when it gets messy and full of meat.

The restaurant is in an upscale district of Brasilia by the lake. We see the giant, glowing head of a cow from the main highway and pull into the parking lot. One side of the restaurant is windows, and we are given the table with the best view of the water. The chairs are blue velvet, the tables are long slabs of irregular wood, and everyone is dressed in tuxedos. Buffet tables, spilling with food, run the length of the restaurant. The servers are called *passadors*, meat waiters. Dozens of them swirl about us, waving their swords of barbecued animals, waiting for each of us to raise our green flag, the signal to bring more meat please. The *passadors* boast three-foot skewers of speared meat. Their blades are shiny and sharp; they wipe them on a towel hung from the waist after every serving. My father calls for more *picanha*, the house specialty of beef tip sirloin cut so a healthy layer of fat still clings to the meat. He eats and laughs, enjoying the service, sometimes raising his flag just to watch them run and then lowering it just as the server reaches the table. He grabs my mother's flag and waves it for her, too. She holds up her hands to say no, but she eats it anyway and declares it delicious. My father wears his napkin as a child would a bib. It is smeared with sauce and grease and hangs from his neck. When the *passadors* bring out the chicken hearts and livers, a quiet rushes over the room, green flags wave frantically in the air.

I sit in my vegetarian hell and take it all in. I haven't eaten meat in five years and the smell makes me close my eyes and turn away. Like most converts, I have become radical in my righteousness and yet, I am an anomaly in Brazil. In our two years in this country, we will never meet another vegetarian. We are a species alone.

My husband and I gorge on the salads, vegetarian sushi, and buttered garlic rolls. We don't declare our vegetarianism. We don't try to explain that we don't eat meat. We keep our flags tucked away in a kind of surrender. We have learned to just stop asking. We have learned that our way of being is foreign here. We don't protest. We just learn to accept Brazil for the way it is, and we learn that our place in it is silence.

In my dream tonight I will jump up on top of this table in my high heels, waving my butter knife in the air and scream, "Eu sou vegetariana! Não como carne!" The *passadors* and my parents will laugh in unison.

The Fool Tree
Willliam Trowbridge

Poof! Like that,
he's rooted thirty feet
into the seventh green,

feeling the chilly nudge
of worms, the tickle
of mole whiskers and

assorted cilia. Has he
blown his birdie? Where
did his five iron go?

Where, for God's sake,
did his arms, his eyes, his
you-know-what?

Maybe he should have tried
a mashie. Does Blue Cross
cover acute rooting?

He doesn't care. *Why
move from this spot*
he wonders, *ever?*

*Why not dine
on the seasons? waltz
in the tuck of breezes?*

tango in gales?
His skin's gnarled
hard enough to blunt

any slur or worry.
His twiggy pate
will leaf out

every year. *Tall,*
he muses, *Ancient,*
Anchored, Majestic,

his thick bark deaf
to the chain saw's
choke and rattle.

The Incredible Shrinking Fool
William Trowbridge

Mountain lion! thinks Fool, just before he sees
it's Snuggles. When he stands, he's eye-to-eye
with the TV. The carpet pile's ankle deep,

moving toward his shins. "EEK," he Minnie Mouses,
music to Snuggles, who hears an evening meal
in the pile of clothes where his master stood.

Fool's now lost in the Grand Canyon
of his left loafer. 9 D, say colossal imprints
on the east wall, which smells like feet.

Then he falls through the molecules
of the sole, through a hydrogen atom,
then a quark, till he's a nano-step from God,

who, unknown to many, is infinitely small
as well as large and wise and good
and never to be told he seems

a lot taller in the Bible or on TV,
as Fool remarks. But, since infinitely small
implies nonentity, God feels free here

not to act the big shot, even suggests
Fool call him Peewee and play him
in a round of miniature golf. Tired

of omnipotence, Peewee offers to play
for the CEO-ship of the cosmos, then designs
to triple bogey the first five holes.

After the game, when Fool's sworn in,
the meek finally do inherit the earth.
For a while, even gluttons and bullies

find themselves saying "May I?"
and "After you." Everyone's a guest,
sipping bubbly at a rose-tinted window,

till Peewee, who dearly misses his toadies
and hit lists, harangues those milquetoasts
into worshipping the ground he scurries over.

As the trumpet of doom dumps its sour note
into the milk and honey, the rich regain
their leverage, the poor requeue for crusts.

It's back to square one, almost, with God
in his ShoeLifts and Fool unright with the world,
this time down to the remotest lepton,

though nobody gives much weight
to God's pronouncements anymore,
he's so small, and his tinny voice such a pain.

Meat and 3 Veg
Michael Cohen

Tell me what you eat and I will tell you what you are.
– Brillat-Savarin, *The Physiology of Taste* (1826)

IF YOU WANT a plate lunch in the little college town of Murray, Kentucky, you go to Rudy's on the court square, Roberson's Hihburger on Route 121 south of town, or Martha's on Route 641 north of town. Be warned that each is a smoking establishment and the strongest drink you can order is the iced tea—you will be asked whether you like it "sweet or unsweet." The plastic glasses in which the tea is served are clear for the unsweetened variety, tea-colored for the sweetened, so that the waitresses, who often refill your glass, will know which to give you.

Rudy's has eighteen square Formica tables and six stools crowded at the counter. In wintertime it's a tight squeeze for the diners, who are often large anyway, and their fat winter coats. Behind a separate, higher counter is the cash register, and behind the register is a cold case with the day's pies. The popular meringues and cream pies are probably Rudy's main claim to uniqueness among Murray's plate-lunch parlors. These days there is always a sugar-free dessert choice as well. When Rudy's is full at peak breakfast and lunch hours, eighty people may be masticating or waiting. The wait is short: usually a plate lunch arrives within about four minutes after the waitress takes the order. If the owner, Dana Anderson (Rudy sold the place to her years ago) is in the tiny kitchen cooking, the wait may be even shorter. And no one is sitting around after eating; if you're finished and you don't move, you will be shoo'd out. Charging two dollars for breakfast and five for lunch, Rudy's depends on turning over those eighteen tables and six stools.

If you choose a plate lunch—and most do—you can put together a vegetarian meal of four selections, but the usual combination is one meat and three vegetables. The meats at Rudy's include honey-glazed ham, liver (beef liver rather than calves' liver, served with onions and gravy), and meat loaf, but the standard fare is chicken with a sage dressing or with dumplings, tenderloin—that is, pork tenderloin cooked in a flour batter, roast beef (dry-roasted and pulled or cut into small pieces), and "country-fried steak," which turns out to be ground beef cooked "chicken-fried," that is, with a flour and egg batter. Some variant of the "country-fried" or "chicken fried" or "breaded beef pattie" shows up on all the menus in town. On Fridays there are fish options, again cooked in a flour or corn-meal batter. The salmon patty is always there on Fridays, and two-piece or three-piece fish dinners with hush puppies, fried potatoes, and slaw—a fish and three veg without the choices. I like to go on Fridays not for the fish, but because liver and onions is always on the menu that day, and one of the vegetable choices is lima beans. My wife abhors this combination, so I don't get it at home.

Rudy's has one vegetable selection you won't see anywhere else in town: the tomato relish. Tomatoes are chopped with onion and jalapeño peppers and served in vinegar with a little sugar to take the bite out. Otherwise, the vegetables are much the same as those served elsewhere in town. The whole-kernel corn, creamed corn, and lima beans are much as they come from the can. With other varieties of peas and beans—purple hull peas, black-eyed peas, pintos, and white beans—a little salt pork or ham usually seasons the dish. Mashed potatoes, always called "cream potatoes" or "creamed potatoes," show up on the menus of all these restaurants every day, and are served with gravy. Buttered carrots, green beans, beets served hot, cabbage wedges—all of these are cooked up with some sugar, although the waitress puts a bottle of vinegar down on the table with the cabbage. Vinegar is also served with turnip greens, though these are not usually sweetened. Sauerkraut is not a usual menu item in this part of the country, but occasionally will show up with Polish sausage among the meat selections. Sweetness is the dominant flavor, followed closely by salt. And you will often see fried green tomatoes on the menus of these places.

The odd thing about the plate-lunch restaurants is their sameness. There are small variations in standard dishes, and there are specialty dishes to be found at each restaurant, but otherwise there is a kind of uniformity that McDonald's quality control guardians would find enviable. Of course there are differences. Roberson's Hihburger (no one now knows why the "g" was left out of the name) and Martha's feature barbecue every day. The barbecue in this part of the country almost always is pork, though a few diners also offer barbecued mutton. Unlike the Texas wet barbecue, slathered with viscous red sauce while cooking, the meat in Tennessee and Kentucky is dry-roasted in small smokehouses behind the restaurant or in cookers made of steel drums. It's pulled apart when done and served with pepper sauces of varying piquancy. The typical barbecue sandwich comes with clumps of the tender meat on a hamburger bun, often topped with slaw. At Roberson's you can also sometimes get a barbecued pork chop as your meat selection on the plate lunch. Martha's serves barbecued ribs as well.

Roberson's offers the cole slaw familiar in all these places—chopped cabbage with a little carrot in a creamed, sweet sauce—along with two other choices: vinegar slaw, which is chopped cabbage with a little chopped bell pepper in diluted vinegar sweetened with sugar, and vinegar slaw with Splenda, for the weight-conscious or the diabetic. Music plays in

Roberson's—a radio station playing country music. Roberson's register is behind the counter in this crowded room with eight booths around the exterior, large-windowed walls and only four places at the counter.

Martha's, the newest of the plate-lunch places, was started in 1986. Martha is a well-kept blonde woman in her fifties with short hair and a fondness for gold jewelry. The local AM radio station WNBS broadcasts a morning show from this restaurant, and two tables on the highway side are marked off for this purpose. Here a roll of paper towels on an upright holder in the middle of each table acknowledges that the ribs and the fried chicken will need to be eaten with the fingers. You can get lasagna for a meat choice here, or ham shank; a selection not usually seen elsewhere is smoked turkey, which often appears on the menu. The "smothered pork chop" is covered with a milk gravy with mushrooms. Martha's is the most spacious of the plate lunch places, with 15 booths and another dozen tables—in all, space for over a hundred people. The kitchen is also the largest, and your plate lunch comes back from it almost as soon as your order has been placed.

Murray residents eat at all three restaurants, but they have favorites, and the customer base at each place depends on its location. The clientele at Rudy's always includes some lawyers and clerks from the nearby courthouse and municipal or county offices. You will also see a sprinkling of downtown merchants, a stockbroker, and the eastside farmers who began going there in the fifties, when Rudy's 99-cent breakfast was the draw.

Roberson's patrons are primarily workmen from the plumbing shop, the lumberyard, the car-repair garages and the other businesses of the "industrial" southwest corner of town, but southside farmers also come in, as do a few young families. The college people—staff and faculty alike—are more likely to show up at Rudy's or Martha's than Roberson's, and few students frequent any of these restaurants, probably because the nearest one is a mile from campus and the crowds in all three have little in common with students in age or interests. Kids who grew up in Murray still come of course, and sometimes bring their friends to see a little bit of local color. Martha's group is the most eclectic because it's on the main north-south highway through town and draws an ever-new population from the transients. She also has regulars among the northside merchants and the county people who live north of town.

Wherever you go, your meat and three veg will be served on a plate divided into three sections, made either of plastic (Martha's) or crockery (Rudy's and Roberson's); the third vegetable will be in a small bowl placed with the meat in the largest section of the plate. You will be offered a choice of rolls or cornbread, or one of each. In the Murray plate-lunch parlors, dessert is a vegetable—that is, you may choose one of the day's featured desserts as one of your three vegetable choices. It is important, I think, during the short wait for your plate to be set in front of you, as you set your taste toward the meal to come, that you remember that dessert is a vegetable. At Rudy's it will be Jell-O or a cobbler or, occasionally, strawberry shortcake that's listed with the vegetable choices on the plate lunch menu. The featured pies cost extra.

Finally, of course, the plate lunch places *are* the town and embody its features: a love of predictability, a surface sweetness free from irony, a resistance to change, a dash of originality in a barrel of the familiar, an attitude about food that it should be cheap, plentiful, and accompanied by tobacco but not alcohol. ■

The Winter Saint
Sandy Longhorn

Freezing suits the sorrowful bones
of this craven saint.
                        What is ice-thick
can be passed over and forgotten.

No shame in a shrine gone barren,

in the saint himself worshipping
an arctic wind
                that picks
the relics clean, scattering the last

of the ancient petitioners.

The weight of their prayers is more
than he can bear
                        when no one
remembers that once he carried honey

and loaves of warm bread to the enemy.

In the Winter Garden

Sandy Longhorn

The supplicant kneels at the stone bench
and wields wild prayers against the frozen air.

When the ice begins in his extremities and seeps
as if called to the core, he clutches close the reliquary

containing the hundred mockingbird hearts
found when they pierced the bloated chest

of the winter saint. The miracle is this sufficient heat
the box gives off when breathed upon in the frost

and the remnant echo of a hundred heartbeats
steady and sure as his once unshakeable faith.

Having Been Entrusted With Safekeeping
Sandy Longhorn

She teaches the brood of black-haired boys
to suspect the lingering vine and its shock
of ruby flowers. Small bursts of flame
she labels poison, making the sign of the cross
in the air over their up-turned eyes.

Kneeling, they learn math at the coffee table,
pencils filled with soft lead. Fat calculations
they use to cipher the difference in the weight
of a blonde-haired angel and the speed of a train
loaded with a decade's worth of sin unleashed.

They translate the bark of the yellow dog
into *fear*, into *danger*. One bite blooms
a red thistle on the skin, a litany of blood knots.
She takes advantage of the fact that each small
trauma nudges them closer to redemption.

Crouching in the Body's Dusty Ruins

Sandy Longhorn

In the hour of wasplight, she allows no sound
to trespass her tongue willed to stone,
breathes in the broken song of the crow

and the cricket interwoven, builds a nest
of aluminum threads in her throat
and settles the chipped pieces of the story there.

Archivist and archaeologist of her own mysteries,
each version begins with the renting asunder.
She is adept at collecting the bloody shards,

the hidden scars, the fragments of each
newly unburied language. Every excavation
ends when she ciphers out the one constant,

the syllables for lust and loss, the names
for a pair of gods hip-joined and ruling
from a constellation of dwindling stars.

The Consolation of Wind
Todd Davis

In the barn, as she helps her husband,
her belly bumps against the worn wood
of stanchions, the warm sides of cows
whose udders are tugged by rubber
and metal, whose milk runs the length
of the barn in a maze of plumbing.
She is tired and her back aches.
She uses fistfuls of bag balm
to ease the skin's stretching, child
kicking her insides as she shovels
manure and hoses the dairy parlor's
slick gutters. Like Perpetua
who was gored by a bull only to become
the patron saint of cows, this woman
is grateful for the neglected beauty
of bovine: fullness of breast, width
and curve of haunch, the strength
of sloped shoulders, the heavy eyes
that watch for the consolation of wind
as it moves in the limbs of lilac
and dogwood.

Vigil
Todd Davis

We stand over this child and watch the waters
roil, mud surfacing, bluebottle flies boiling
around ears, collecting at the seat of his pants.

This is the body we've made, the sweet juice
of love's temptation, a split tomato: yellow
seeds in pink water. Like rain caught in a bucket,

like sunlight pushed flat against tin, I am trying
not to forget how our son spilled into the hands
of that first day. I suppose what's left is to settle in,

to listen to the mortal-song the body sings.
We shouldn't be surprised flesh chants as it does
the work of the body: rain pooling in spent cornfields,

a small boy fluttering as if pinned to a clothesline.
Here's what we have left to learn: when the earth
drops away beneath us, we can't help but fall.

Crash Zoom
Angela Delarmente

WITH MY VIDEO camera, I film Mom standing in the bathroom doorway and observing my sister like a gentle warden. "Hurry," she says, preventing Lourdes from teasing her bangs another inch higher. "He's here. You have to go."

I can hear Dad clearing his throat in the living room. He's all pleated Dockers, polo shirts, and boat shoes these days. He carries the trace scent of Irish Spring and cigarettes, but I don't forget his old smell—whiskey as aftershave. He's here for me and Lourdes; he has us every other weekend.

Lourdes puts her Aqua Net canister down then outlines her lips with bruise-colored liner. "Where you got to be that's so important?"

Mom answers by tugging at the shirt of her nursing scrubs. "I just want him out my living room. Can't he just wait in the car and honk?"

I pull out for a wide shot of Lourdes' face, but as she passes me she covers the camera lens like a stalked celebrity.

When we go into the living room, Dad stands up from the couch. "Okay then," he says to Mom. "I'll drop them off Sunday?"

Mom nods. "Be good, girls," she says to Lourdes and me.

Lourdes stomps out of the house and Dad follows her with his series of chipper, rapid-fire questions she ignores or vaguely answers.

Before I leave, Mom says, "Gaby—if things get too weird—"

"Things are always too weird. Besides, he's on the *fifth step*. He's almost halfway to *cured*." She grabs my air-quoting fingers and kisses them. She knows tonight we'll be meeting Gloria, Dad's new white girlfriend.

Mom comes at me from another angle. "I just want you to try, okay?" She fusses with my hair while I put away my video camera. "Because he's paying for you guys now. And he's helping us out." She leans into me and watches Dad put our weekend bags into the trunk of his car. "And he's looking all right, I think. He's cleaning up."

Outside, Dad's car idles; Lourdes sulks in the back seat. I tell Mom, "It's Lourdes you should be worried about."

~~~

When we were younger Lourdes always called shotgun. But these days she's in the backseat with her headphones on. She is sunk so far down that when I turn around all I see is the top of her chola bangs, styled like a Latina gangster's. Her ratted bangs come up from her hairline and curl back like a wave, a black conch shell.

"Hey, Lourdy," Dad says. He looks at her reflection in the rearview mirror. "You using the pool? I sent Efrem over there to clean it."

Lourdes doesn't answer. I tell him, yes, the pool's fine. And yes, I was there when Efrem came last week. I tell him I swim sometimes but Lourdes never does; this, I don't tell him. She doesn't like to be bare and wouldn't do anything that would compromise her hair, her makeup. She used to love to swim; I don't forget this about her. When I look at her new self long enough, I remember three summers ago, late afternoon by the pool.

Dad sits at a foldout table playing poker. The other players are mostly pinoys—janitors, nurses' aides, medical transcriptionists from Saint Jude's where Dad is an orderly. Every now and again, one of the men swats a fly with the t-shirt he has just shed.

"Hoy, pare!" a man says to Dad. "Pass the tsitsaron!" Dad reaches for a bowl of Filipino-style pork rinds, but he fumbles and the crispy, pale curls pop into the air and rain down on the cards and poker chips. Someone throws a pork rind at my father, and everyone groans but no one is really upset. They keep on with their game, occasionally dusting crumbs from the table and passing around appetizer plates of lumpia and barbequed chicken.

Mom hums to herself while she muddles mint and lime for another round of mojitos. She goes into the house for more meat to put on the grill. Everyone watches the poker game, but no one's really interested unless the stakes are raised, or someone breaks bank. Arms like brooms push and sweep stacks of colored playing chips across the table.

Above the pool, Lourdes, in a white bikini like wisps of wet tissue paper, waves from the edge of the diving board. The swimmers wade to the side, block the sun from their eyes, and wait. Everyone watches. Dad, sunglasses askew, raises his rocks glass to her. Who is cheering louder? Dad or Damien, the twenty-year-old boy with the strong chin but weak mustache who used to sweep floors at Saint Jude's? I feel a pang of jealousy because Damien, with whom I'm a little infatuated, is smitten with my big sister Lourdes. But then he taps me on the shoulder and whispers, "She'll have to do a hell of a lot better than your cannonball, that's for sure." I have a premonition—Damien and I get married when I graduate from high school.

Lourdes gives the board a few bounces. Then she leaps. Her body is a sleek silhouette against the sun, a black brushstroke arcing into turquoise water. Wild clapping erupts before she breaks the surface. She emerges, and for a flash, she looks terrified and gasps for air. She wipes the water from her eyes, sees my father, sees Damien, then beams. "Perfect Ten! Perfect Ten!" Dad says, spilling his drink.

Mom comes out of the kitchen holding a pair of bloody steaks. "What is it? What'd I miss?"

Dad asks if she could spot him a twenty. She says, "You know better than to ask."

Efrem pulls a bill from his wallet and tosses it to Dad. "For Lourdes' Perfect Ten, *pare*. Pay the lady back if you win." Efrem winks at Mom. She shakes her head and goes to the grill.

Later, the party finale: Dad dives off the roof and into the pool. It takes us awhile to realize he has a mild concussion. He is so drunk, he doesn't know he's hit his head against the pool floor, or lost the gold inlay on his left molar.

~~~

Dad tells us about Gloria: "I met her at the meetings. Nice lady, a good person. Smart, too. She's been going to meetings for ten years. Did I tell you guys? She's a stylist? She does hair and stuff. Lourdy, you'll like her. She knows all about colors, skin, hair. She already told me she'd be happy to give you guys a cut. You know, for back-to-school?"

Lourdes turns up her headphones. I look at Dad's hair and have to admit—it's salon quality. He's got pomade in there, and the fade on the back of his head is looking subtle and well kept.

"We've got time before dinner. What do you guys want to do? How about the mall? You need back-to-school clothes?"

How Lourdes hears him through the headphones, I'm not sure. She says, "Go to the Galleria. Towne Center's lame."

~~~

We walk the length of the Galleria and say nothing. Every now and again, Dad stops at a kiosk and picks up a novelty item. We watch a sales woman bedazzle a pair of jeans with a rhinestone gun. When Dad sees we aren't interested, he wanders over to the Scribble Me This kiosk and we watch a demonstration of the Scribbler—a pen on a spinning top that, when twirled on a paper pad, draws dizzying and pointless little hurricanes.

Lourdes wanders over to the Asian gifts kiosk where there are several models of Mini Zen Gardens—shallow boxes filled with fine sand, bonsai trees, and miniature rakes. I look into one of the Gardens and see LOR-D, Lourdes' tagging moniker, drawn into the sand by one of her maroon press-on nails.

Now she's over at the calligraphy tablets—the kind you draw on with a brush dipped in water. The writing turns ghostly then evaporates, leaving behind a clean slate.

She paints a cock-and-balls on the tablet.

"You're sick, Lourdy," I say.

"What? Like you haven't seen one?" she says. "Whatevs, prudence."

After she adds spiky pubes to the balls and puts the brush down, the clerk comes by and removes the tablet from the easel. Lourdes is smug. She smiles at him and with her slightly crossed front teeth, pushes and pulls the sterling barbell pierced through her tongue. The clerk hesitates, studies her mouth for a second, then moves the cock-and-balls tablet to a shelf under his till. He goes back to arranging the plastic Buddha coin banks.

Dad gives up on kiosks and instead focuses on any store selling young women's fashions—anything with bright lights, oontz-oontz-oontz beats and diva vocals pumping out of the store speakers. In front of each store, he pauses and asks if we want to check it out.

"I need bras," Lourdes says. She swaggers across the corridor to Frederick's of Hollywood. We follow the shuffle and scrape of her Nikes and her khaki pant cuffs against the polished floor. She looks like a joke to me, like a kid dressed as a gangstress for Halloween—her button-up shirt worn open (except for the top-most button) exposing her tight, white wifebeater, hemmed at the navel. Considering her boyish chola phase, it's any wonder what she wants from Frederick's. Last time we came here with Dad, Lourdes was still goth; she bought corsets and a few flavors of fishnet stockings.

She made the leap from goth to chola around the end of the school year after she annoyed her vampire friends by slicing superficial cuts on her palms and faking stigmata. They said she exploited the style, took things too far; she claimed she was too hardcore for them, those posers. Now she hangs with some wannabe Westsiders and spends our non-dad weekends tagging the walls of the train underpass and drinking malt-liquor with the cholo crowd from the high school near the barrio. It takes her an hour to get there by bus, but sometimes she wheedles Mom into dropping her off here, at the mall, where she meets a boy who pedals her to the other side of the tracks on the handles of his low-rider bicycle.

Her transformation involved shedding the black (but keeping the ghostly makeup) and trading it for khaki, white, touches of gang blue— blue bandanas, blue underwear peeking out the waist of her pants, and sometimes a blue tear drawn at the corner of her left eye. I've overheard her phone conversations—she's "working up the *cojones* to get it inked for real."

When Mom caught Lourdes in the bathroom taking close-up Polaroids of herself and her faux tear tattoo, I was walking down the hallway shooting random scenes of the house with my video camera. I decided to keep it running.

I went in for a close-up of Mom. "Ay *nako!*" she said to Lourdes, "You're not even Mexican!"

I zoomed out so they were both in frame and said, "She's hoping our last name passes for Latino. She wants to be a chola."

"You should be ashamed! You know, we share the same last name as the Philippine's National Hero!" Mom, mouth pulled into an angry bud, looked into the camera then turned back to Lourdes.

"Can I get some damn privacy?"

I crash zoomed onto Lourdes' face, her tear tattoo.

"Man, get that shit out of my grill!" She threw a hair brush at me before slamming the bathroom door in our faces. I kept rolling.

Mom said, "I'm just saying, don't act like who you aren't. What if they think you're one of them? What if you get shot!" She launched into one of her cautionary tales, which all end with someone getting drug-addicted, raped, pregnant, incarcerated, and eventually, capped. In her stories, someone always dies or is slowly dying of AIDS or some other viral disease on the verge of mutation.

"Lourdes, I'm not done. I want to talk about this."

"Why don't you stop acting like you know what you're talking about!" Lourdes said behind the door. We could hear her shuffling products on the shelves and in the drawers. "You better turn off that camera, Gaby, or I swear to God."

Close-up of Mom's hand jiggling the door handle—locked. "*Hoy!* Lourdes, open up."

"You're goddamn clueless," Lourdes said. "You always have your head up your goddamn ass."

Mom looked at the camera, her face blanched and her chin quivering. "Gaby, goddamn it," Mom said. "Not now."

~~~

At Frederick's, Lourdes snatches up black bras and tube tops while Dad and I linger near the shop entrance. After each bra Lourdes tries on, she comes out of her dressing room and checks herself at a communal mirror to make sure the bra outline is visible under her thin wifebeater. Why the mirror in the dressing room isn't good enough for this body check seems beyond the other customers, but it makes Dad uncomfortable, so I suppose it's a good enough reason for her. When she comes out wearing a tube top, Dad turns around and faces the mall corridor. He and I stand with our heads dead straight, like we're a couple of men pissing at a urinal.

Dad tilts his head in my direction and without looking at me says, "Excited for school?"

"Sure," I say.

"Going into high school, yeah?"

"No, I started already. Last year."

"Oh, right."

"Yeah, I'm going into tenth."

Dad whistles. "Tenth grade!"

We watch a gaggle of kids dressed in animal costumes. They tug the hands of their adult chaperones and head for a children's event at the mall cineplex. Among them is a woman holding the paw of a little girl dressed as a lion. The lion cub looks up at us and roars.

The woman says, "Tell them you're not a scary lion."

"It's okay. I won't eat you," the little girl says. Distracted by the colorful and twirling wind chimes at the Misty Mountains kiosk, she bounds away. The woman sighs, smiles in the name of parental solidarity. Dad says, "She won't eat you now, but get back to me when she's sixteen."

He meant this to be funny, to connect with a fellow parent, but it comes out all wrong. The woman's smile flatlines. She goes after the little lion, rescues her from the tangle of a windsock's rainbow ribbons.

"You still interested in movies and all that?" Dad says.

"Uh-huh," I say, crossing and uncrossing my arms.

"Efrem was telling me about you the other day. When he came to the house to clean the pool, he said you were sitting on the roof with your camera and asked if you could shoot him cleaning it."

"Yeah, it's just a thing. Just a project."

Lourdes comes singing out of the dressing room. She brings her mountain of items to the checkout counter—Dad's cue to join her and get out his credit card. While each scant item is scanned and bagged, Lourdes pulls out a pink thong from a bin of discounted underwear. "Maybe we should get this for Gloria," she says. I shake my head and Dad pretends not to hear her. "I'm *kidding*," Lourdes says. She sling-shoots the thong back into the bin. A few customers knit their brows and cast sideways, judgmental eyes in our direction. Their reactions seem lost on Dad, who just smiles and charges everything without a beat.

Back in the mall corridor, Dad looks at Lourdes and says, "Those pants are the big thing, huh? The style?" He looks down at her khakis: creases sharp enough to cut paper; the low waist cinched with a long fabric belt, the excess of which droops from the clamp-on buckle halfway down her thigh. "You could fit another person in those."

"I know, I've tried," Lourdes says. She heads toward Life Uniform where they sell scrubs, construction wear, unadorned sweatsuits and t-shirts. She picks up three pairs of Dickies workpants in navy, maroon, black.

Dad says to me, "Why don't you get a few things?"

I pick out some sweatshirts and head into the dressing room. Lourdes, in the room next to me, sings with abandon. *Can you pay my telephone bills? Do you pay my automo' bills?*

Everything reminds me of our bedroom closet, a surrogate womb that I hid in whenever my folks fought, or Lourdes was mad at me. Sometimes I'd go in there for a little privacy and screen the footage I'd filmed or flip through the *Hustler* mags I'd stolen from Dad. The night of the pool party was the last time I hid in the closet. I should've known I'd end up there when Dad gave me his camcorder. He was drunk and afraid he'd break it.

I see myself small at the kitchen entrance, filming Mom at the sink. She's strangling silverware with a sponge and drowning plates under the faucet. I've been recording for two, three minutes when Dad comes into the kitchen from the patio. "Where's your purse? I need twenty to stay in the game."

She shuts off the water and glares at him. "But you already borrowed from Efrem."

I fix the camera for an over-the-shoulder shot, framing Mom's back with Dad facing her. He turns to the party outside. "They're waiting. Where's your purse?"

"You promised," Mom says.

The light is good in the kitchen, but I don't want to see this. With the camera's eyepiece butted against my face, I walk out of the kitchen unnoticed and into the backyard. They grow large as I approach: Lourdes and Damien sitting at the pool edge, their feet kicking in the water. I angle the camera down at Lourdes. She looks up and sighs at me. Damien nudges her and sticks his tongue out, does the disappearing thumb trick where it looks like he's detaching it from his hand. He is thin and androgynous, even with wispy facial hair. He pushes himself up from the pool ledge and I train the camera on him as he goes to refill his drink.

Lourdes says, "Would you give me some room here? Just for once?"

"I'm not even doing anything, God," I say. "I'm just here."

"That's the problem."

I zoom close on Damien filling two cups with mojitos. A young woman comes into frame. Damien leans into her neck, but she pushes his forehead away and calls him *gago*, stupid; she walks away, laughing. I hear Lourdes stir the water. She pulls my arm down and takes the camera. "I'm older than you, so who you think he's going to go for?"

We always share everything, even if we do so grudgingly, but Damien is different. I take the camera back, turn it on Lourdes and frame her in a series of Dutch Tilts, which I later learn is a cheap tactic for conjuring physical and mental tension. It's my way of crowding her from a distance, of letting her know I'm there.

"Come on, Gaby. Leave us alone." In the frame, she makes a scooting motion, then her eyes break from the camera's gaze and follow Damien. He comes back to her, and back into my view, with a drink in each hand. He sips from one cup, hands the other to Lourdes. I feel a kink in my chest.

I leave, but shoot them from a distance. The soft waves churning in the water refract the pool lights and cast shimmering, snaking white ribbons on their bodies. They come in and out of focus, sidle closer until their hips touch. Damien talks against Lourdes' neck. When he runs his finger over her shoulder and down her arm, I shiver.

"I used to tell myself something about you," I hear Mom say to Dad. They are still in the kitchen. "I used to say 'At least he's a happy drunk.'"

When I go back inside, I steady the camcorder on Dad. He's leaning on the counter, and vacantly wagging his brows at the camera.

"Sweetheart," Mom says. "Give it to me before you break it." Her hand grows larger in the frame until it covers the lens and takes away the camcorder. "Don't record what we'll only cry about later."

"I'm going upstairs," I say, brooding. I tear a napkin from the paper towel roll and grab a couple of cold ribs from a plate on the counter.

"Night, love," Dad says. He goes back outside with a wrinkled twenty in hand.

I sit in our bedroom closet and eat the ribs. My own chewing and slopping fills my ears and mutes the party noises outside. I tug on the long pull-chain dangling from the ceiling and in the dark, with only the light from the bedroom window pushing through the closet slats, my thoughts narrow on the growing distance between me and everyone else. Even Lourdes is far away. Just this morning we painted each other's toenails and drew tattoos—hearts pierced with arrows—on each other's forearms. I tell myself, Let her have Damien. See who she runs to when he breaks her heart.

~~~

After we finish shopping, we go to the food court and stop at Chan's because Lourdes says she's hungry.

Dad looks at his watch. Courageously, he says, "Are you sure you can't wait? We've only got an hour and some change until dinner, you might ruin your appetite." I think she might pull a Veruca Salt—jump onto the counter and demand the golden eggroll—but she just looks past him and clutches her bare midriff.

"Just a snack then. Something light."

Dad and I get eggrolls. Lourdes gets a dragon-sized meal which I know she doesn't really want but orders anyway. She takes two bites of General Tso's, eats the steamed dumpling and ignores her fried rice. She announces she's full but as we leave the food court, she talks a twenty from Dad to pay for a frou frou ice-coffee drink. She pockets the change, drinks half, then tosses it out. I look for signs of disapproval from Dad, but see no bulging temples or stiff jaw.

He stops at a kiosk selling psych-out optical posters with the hidden pictures. He concentrates on a poster with a purple frame around a fuzzy pattern like white and black ash. He says, "Hoy, it's the *Last Supper*. You guys see that? There's Judas and Jesus and everything." Lourdes burps and heads for a store called Icing where they've got two-for-one on hoop earrings.

~~~

Dad whistles in the mall parking lot. He says, "Are we Kool and the Gang? Did you get everything you wanted?"

I say thanks and give him a wimpy hug. Lourdes blows a huge bubblegum bubble and lets it pop inches away from his face.

While Dad puts our purchases in the trunk, Lourdes and I get in the car and I ask her what her fucking problem is. She whispers back—go to hell, traitor. She shakes her walkman, but the CD inside doesn't turn. The batteries are out of juice.

We drive and Dad turns on the radio, fixes the dial to the college station. He looks at Lourdes in the rearview. "This okay? You guys still listen to this?"

I see Lourdes in the side mirror, chomping gum.

"It's fine," I say.

"It's your car," Lourdes adds.

Dad smiles, clicks on the blinker, turns the car left onto the main drag. To Lourdes he says, "Not for long. She's all yours when you graduate."

"What?" I say. "No way." I turn around to Lourdes and mouth, Oh, my God! She mocks me, then leans her forehead against the window pane and looks out at the shopping centers, rolling, rolling away.

Dad says to me, "Don't worry. You won't need a car when you go to NYU."

"That's three years away," I say, "so who knows."

"Oh, you'll get in and you'll make your movies. I have a good feeling. I pray for it." I fight the urge to grin, and turn away so he doesn't see me. I look back at Lourdes in the sideview and shelve my smile.

Dad is still unaccustomed to Lourdes' new phase. He doesn't realize it's no longer soundtracked by moody songs with backdrops of discordant guitars and plinky synthesizers bemoaning the inner-prison in each of us. She's moved on to another equally moody phase with its own sort of bleakness—the streets, money, bitches and hoes, 5-0—threaded by thick beats and bass-lines that settle like milk in the gut.

On the radio, Morrissey croons that he hasn't had a dream in a long time. Dad awkwardly bobs his head; he's offbeat, slapping his thumb against the steering wheel.

Without irony or sarcasm he says, "This stuff is breaking my heart."

Lourdes, who can't stand when she thinks he pretends to like things, replaces a battery from her walkman with one from Dad's mini-flashlight rolling along the backseat floor. She hits play and the snap of the snare, the thud of the bass drum leak from her headphones and argue with the treble-heavy radio vocals. The air turns muddy. Lourdes glares at Dad, but he acts Zen, lets her hate-gaze roll over him like mist.

~~~

At the steakhouse, before the bread and drinks arrive, Gloria presents us with gifts. She hands us packages swathed in white tissue and wrapped with silky pink ribbon as if they're virgin sacrifices. The presents are a transparent attempt to gain our favor, but I don't blame her. Lourdes is scary with all the black goop around her eyes, her angry arched brows, and huge gold earrings like Chinese throwing stars.

I peel back the tissue and see a red suede diary. In gold-leafed cursive, the word *Secrets* is embossed on the cover, the esses spilling over the sides. The suede is soft; I run my hand over the embossing as if reading Braille. A gift card for Gazer's Camera and Video Supply falls onto my lap when I open the book.

"For your movies," Dad says.

For Lourdes' sake, I thank Gloria with dampened enthusiasm.

Lourdes tears open her gift—a heavy cross with fake crystals set into the father, the son, and each shoulder of the holy ghost. The cross hangs on chunky silver links, thick as dog's chain.

"You got some blings," Dad says.

I cringe for him, even Gloria does.

Lourdes lets the chain links fumble through her fingers like a handful of boring pebbles, but I know she secretly loves the necklace because she's been lusting after it ever since Inez Cruz pointed it out in *Cosmo Girl*. The necklace was featured in a photo spread titled "What's Your Narrative?" Lourdes drops the necklace, cross first, back in the box.

She regresses. She chews with her mouth open and speaks in Pig Latin. "*Asspay ethay utterbay*," she says to me.

"Ooh! I know this," Gloria says. She thinks for a moment and takes her time to say, "*O-nay oblemp-ray*." She reaches across me, picks up the ramekin of butterballs and offers it to Lourdes, but Lourdes doesn't take it. Instead she moves onto Spanish, but it turns out Gloria knows a little herself.

"*Come mierda*," Lourdes says.

Dad tells her to mind herself, to please speak English, that it's rude not to in front of Gloria. "I'm sorry about this," he says to her.

He points his fork at Lourdes. "What are you? Twelve?"

Gloria wipes her lips with her napkin and darts her eyes around the restaurant. Only Dad is eating. He's sawing at his rare steak and swabbing bite-sized pieces with mashed potatoes. The surrounding restaurant—its mahogany tables, roving busboys, and dining guests—seems to stretch and extend the way light speed around spaceships is rendered in movies. But our table is still and heavy, and somewhere behind us, waitstaff sing *Happy Birthday* to a customer.

Lourdes throws her napkin at Dad and calls him a white wash. She pushes from the table and thunders away. I get up to follow her, but Dad puts his hand on my shoulder and says, "Don't."

"I don't know what to say. I'm so sorry," he says to Gloria.

"It's okay." She pats his hand. "Go ahead."

"Maybe this was too soon?"

Gloria shakes her head, waves as if shooing a fly—no big deal. But I see the downward tug at the corners of her mouth. Dad asked if it was too soon, but I think it might be too late. With Lourdes things always feel too late. Dad gets up from the table and goes after her.

"I know what she must be thinking," Gloria says. An embarrassed pink rises from her neck to her temples.

"No," I say. "No, you don't."

~~~

If I could tell Gloria what Lourdes must be thinking, I would say she is thinking of all the things that should've happened, instead of the things that actually did.

She is thinking that she should have a different father, a different mother. Or even a different sister.

This sister would be brave enough to walk out of the closet she hides in when Damien gently pushes Lourdes onto her bed with one hand, and turns off the Hello Kitty lamp on the night stand with his other. This sister doesn't play the Peeping Tom, holding her breath against the slats of the closet door. She lets her resentment float up and away—a balloon tugged by the wind. The alarm in her gut takes over her inclination toward invisibility. She takes a deep breath, walks out of the closet, and cock-blocks Damien before he has the chance to coax the bikini off Lourdes.

And when the different Dad Lourdes should've had walks in on her and Damien, he turns into Superman. He drags that boy out to the party for everyone to see, carries him up to the roof and punts him into the pool.

Instead it happens like this: Dad walks past Lourdes' bedroom to the bathroom. He bangs repeatedly on the bathroom door and says, "Damien! You in there? I know you're holding, friend. Give us a pinch!"

Damien has his hand sealed over Lourdes' mouth. He pleads with her, "Shh! Anything, whatever you want." She bites his hand and he yelps. I see their dark shape split into two.

Dad bursts in, bleary and ready to topple. When he flicks on the lights, he looks at them as if they're an optical puzzle—just dark fuzz with a hidden picture underneath. He pulls Lourdes off the ground, slaps her, takes a towel from the floor and throws it at her. Damien apologies as he pulls up his boxers and jeans. He hobbles out of the room and flees the house without his shoes and without so much as a slap on the hand. Lourdes clutches the towel to her front and pushes past Dad. I hear the bathroom door slam and lock, and expect to hear our mother bounding up the stairs but she doesn't come. Is she is in the laundry room, the backyard, or the kitchen pacing between the stove and sink?

I stay in the closet and watch Dad stare at the ground, shifting from foot to foot. "Shit," he says, pawing his way out of the room.

I make my way outside and stand in the backyard with everyone else, our faces lifted toward the first-floor roof. Dad is up there. He holds his palms out as if trying to quiet the crowd, but we're already silent and gaping.

Efrem cups his mouth. "Come on, *pare!* Come down now—it's getting late, it's too high."

"It's just a short way down!" Dad says. "It's not far at all!"

He leaps; we gasp.

~~~

Early in the morning, after Dad had been taken to the ER for the rising goose egg on his head, he sat on the living room couch glancing at Lourdes with shame and disgust. Lourdes cried and Mom's mouth hung open and empty. Every now and then Mom asked for someone to explain what the hell was going on. I lingered in the background, tried to make myself a shadow, but eventually Mom looked at me and ordered me to bed. I went to our room, left the door ajar, and listened to the rise and fall of their muffled voices.

Lourdes came into our room before dawn. She lay on her bed and said, "*He* wanted to." I waited for her to continue but nothing came. There was a terrible clanging of pots and pans coming from the kitchen. I heard Mom call Dad a bastard, a liar, a drunk, a pimp. I lay next to Lourdes, but she kicked me away.

"He wanted to what?" I said, like an idiot. Did she know I was hiding? That I'd seen the whole thing? I stayed silent, thinking the truth would yank her further away from me.

"We were just gonna listen to music, that's all," she said. "It was all *him*. He wanted to."

After Lourdes fell asleep, I padded downstairs to the living room where Dad sat on the couch watching infomercials. He held a bag of ice wrapped in a dishcloth against his head. Though he stared at the television as if I wasn't there, he said, "What Gaby? I have a headache. You need something?"

I tried to use The Force, telepathy, prayer. I felt I had a responsibility—I wanted to tell him what I saw and to relay what Lourdes had told me.

"Are you mad at her?" This was all I could manage.

He kept his eyes on the television and fussed with the ice bag. "I don't know what you mean."

There were no other words about it.

Even though Lourdes and I used to be close, neither one of us broached the incident with the other, not even on the occasions when our closeness seemed rekindled, when she appeared to be safe and content. During those moments we'd be watching a stupid movie or flipping through magazines, commiserating, and recovering from a laughing fit. I would look at her and gather my nerve. Did you know I was there when it happened? I'm sorry I didn't stop it and I'm sorry I didn't tell them what I saw. I planned to say these things, but before I could speak, it seemed she already knew what was coming. She'd look at me as if anticipating fingernails across a chalkboard.

~ ~ ~

Gloria and I avoid meeting each other's eyes. I narrow my line of sight and focus on the empty seat to my left while a busboy refills our four water glasses. I tell her I should go, I'm sorry. She says, don't be. She waves at our server and scribbles into the air for the check.

"Tell your father to call me," she says. I leave her with our cooled steaks, our picked-over dinner rolls. She downs her glass of grape juice as I zip past her.

In middle of the steakhouse parking lot, under a lamppost's yellow beam, my father pleads with Lourdes in low tones. As she pulls away from his grip, her shirt rips. She scrambles to the ground in search of a runaway button. Dad gets a hold of her arms, but she wrestles free and drops back to the ground.

Nearby, a teenage boy sneaks pictures of Lourdes with a disposable camera. She's bent forward, facing him, her chest spilling out her wifebeater as she paws the ground and bits of rock and glass for her button. When the boy winds the roll and snaps another picture, I grit my teeth, pluck a rock by my feet. He notices me and disappears into the parking lot. I intended to intervene—to take the camera from the boy or to break up Lourdes and Dad, but as usual I hang back. I put the rock in my pocket.

Dad gets a hold of Lourdes' arms and pulls her up. She wrenches against him, pushes off his shoulders. "I'm not him, Lourdy," Dad says. "I'm not the same guy." He cradles her head against his chest as if trying to shove her inside of him. "You think I'm not paying for it but I am. I would pay all at once if I could."

They are locked together now, grappling and swaying. And if you didn't see what just happened, if you stand at a different angle or just stare at their shadows, you would think they are dancing. ◾

BOOK REVIEWS

Today I Wrote Nothing: The Selected Writings of Daniil Kharms
Translated From the Russian by Matvei Yankelevich
The Overlook Press, 2009
288 pages
$15.95 (paper)

Reviewed by A.J. Morgan

I first read Daniil Kharms in *The New Yorker*. I have continued to read him because his work is different, fresh, and challenging. It is also ever-changing. To use a cliché, when you read him, expect the unexpected. *Today I Wrote Nothing* contains poetry, short stories, and plays; but don't expect to see them in their usual forms. In his poetry there is little discernable meter and repetition often serves as the only container. His short stories are both slices of life and fractionized accounts that far predate the micro-stories of today. His plays read like a violent version of *Punch and Judy*.

Kharms' work is at once familiar and foreign. As founder (1928) and member of the OBERIU (Association of Real Art) movement, Kharms grounded his work in "absurdism," which preceded the European "Theatre of the Absurd." In the Introduction, the translator Matvei Yankelevich quotes from Kharms' journal:

> *I am interested only in nonsense; only in that which has no practical meaning. Life interests me only in its most absurd manifestation.*

This is not Tolstoy. A better approximation might be Albert Camus—if Camus were funny. Camus' work features a similar stark minimalism about daily events and an absence of the character-driven fiction most readers are habituated to. The stories share a sense of fate with ancient Greek tragedies in which a hero is on a collision course with his destiny, yet having prior knowledge of the outcome changes nothing. Kharms' work is full of collisions, accidental encounters, and chance events:

> *The Meeting*
> *Now, one day, a man went to work, and on the way he met another man, who having bought a loaf of Polish bread, was heading back home where he came from.*
> *And that's it, more or less. (Events)*

This book is made up of a very good introduction, four sections (*Events, The Old Woman, The Blue Notebook,* and *Other Writings*) and useful notes at the end. Both *Events* and *Other Writings* contain collections; *The Old Woman* is a novella, and *The Blue Notebook* a series of twenty-nine micro stories. *The Blue Notebook* also has the distinction of containing the title piece in story number twenty-five:

> Enough of laziness and doing nothing! Open this notebook every day and write down half a page at the very least. If you have nothing to write down, then at least, following Gogol's advice, write down that today there's nothing to write. Always, write with attention and look on writing as a holiday.

After giving this advice Kharms skips story number twenty-six, violating his own rules, while laughing at our expectations. On that day Kharms wrote nothing.

Reading *Events* is a little like reading Lewis Carroll's trip down the rabbit hole. Indeed Carroll was one of Kharms' favorite authors. In one story, *Tumbling Old Women*, a series of curious women tumble out the window and shatter. The first fall reads as a terrible event, yet after seven more, the falls seem repetitive almost mechanical. The odd verb choice, to shatter, is used throughout. In a humorous prose piece titled, *Sonnet*, there is a sequence problem—no one can remember the counting order. *Optical Illusion* reads like slapstick with a man putting on his spectacles and seeing one thing, then taking them off and seeing something else. This act is repeated time and again, until the man in question decides the optical illusion is due to the corrective glasses, since he does not want to believe what he otherwise sees.

What I found most interesting in *The Old Woman* is how the death in the story does not affect the reader as much as the anxiety of the narrator about forgetting to turn his stove off. In Kharms' work, importance often seems placed on the wrong things. Kharms addressed this himself in a story from *Other Writings*:

> **How easy it is for a person to get tangled up** in *insignificant things. You can walk for hours from the table to the wardrobe and from the wardrobe to the couch and never find a way out…*

An unusual number of stories concern food: for example, there are frequent encounters with friends who share vodka, bread, and sausages.

I thought this was unusual until I realized Kharms was not only trying to create an effect, but was actually hungry. His writings were labeled Anti-Soviet and he wrote knowing he would only be able to feed his desk drawer with his efforts.

Daniil Kharms starved to death in prison in 1942 during the Leningrad Blockade. His sense that order and causality were missing in his life proved to be well-founded. In "Today I Wrote Nothing" miracles and magic do not turn out how you expect, and fables don't always deliver meaningful messages.

Wintergirls
by Laurie Halse Anderson
Penguin Group, 2009
278 pages
$9.99 (paper)

Reviewed by Christine Bailey

Much like she did with rape in her best-selling and critically acclaimed novel *Speak* published over a decade ago, Laurie Halse Anderson fearlessly tackles the pressing topic of eating disorders in her new novel *Wintergirls*. Her approach is much the same in both books. She catapults one immediately into the grip of teenage life, revealing the complexities and struggles of adolescence, and she writes with unrestricted truth to and for those afflicted. Because her delivery is credible and powerful, albeit harrowing, her voice is not easily ignored.

The movement of *Wintergirls* is fast, begging the reader to hold on as it shifts into high gear from the start. The novel is written as a first person account. The technique of using sometimes short, abrasive sentences—"I turn off the shower. Clouds hang in the air. Tears roll down the mirror, the walls, and the windows"—proves masterful as it reveals an authentic teen voice. Sometimes more is said between the words, eliciting an active reading. The ironic framework makes this book stand out, as *Speak* did for the same reason. Both books have protagonists unwilling to "speak" about their issues, but their voices are still heard loud and clear.

What is exposed through the narrator's terse language is a teenage girl haunted by the death of her best friend. Both girls were deeply entrenched in a battle to be the thinnest; however, one died as a result of the competition while the other is left behind to cope. Lia is the survivor. In sporadic spurts of internal monologue, we experience the persistent combat of her struggles: "I'm hungry. I need to eat. I hate eating. I need to eat. I hate eating. I need to eat. I love not-eating. The red oil light blinks ON/OFF, ON/OFF, ON/OFF. I shift out of PARK and accelerate." We are confronted by a mind riddled with conflict and a voice choked by despair.

What throws me however, is the section at the back of the novel called "Discussion Questions." I cannot recall Shakespeare giving discussion questions on teen suicide at the close of *Romeo and Juliet*. I'm not sure that the inclusion of talking points is fitting here. Should the narrative not speak for itself? I would argue that Anderson's thought-provoking offering of Lia's struggle is more than sufficient in arousing questions from its audience. The talking points lessen its worth for me.

Putting aside that one reservation and I can easily do so, I ultimately find that *Wintergirls* portrays a "teen girl" expertly. We are taken on a swift ride through adolescent emotion, and what is given to us is a character who resonates long after the ride is over. Lia is someone readers care about. She teaches us about the fragility of life, and she teaches us about what it means to struggle daily. A certain hope is even unveiled in her final words, "I am thawing."

Beg, Borrow, Steal: A Writer's Life
by Michael Greenberg
Other Press, New York, 2009
216 pages
$19.95

Reviewed by Jacqueline J. Kohl

Imagine living on a shoestring as a struggling writer only to learn your procrastination cost you $107,344. If that would make you alternate between depressing verbiage and four-letter epithets, you will as I have, appreciate how Michael Greenberg described that experience and others with amusing pathos and keen observations in *Beg, Borrow, Steal: A Writer's Life*. These stories originally appeared in Greenberg's freelance column in the *Times Literary Supplement* between June 2003 and April 2009. In some ways, the structure of his columns reminds me of the feuilleton. Originally a supplement to political French newspapers consisting of likeable and readable literary escapades, the feuilleton is the current format for the "Talk of the Town" section in *The New Yorker*.

Greenberg's title is literally right on the money. The collection is structured around two basic ideas: the work he (and sometimes friends and family) did to stay financially afloat, or the predicaments that arose from the possession (or lack thereof) of cold cash. The price he paid for each experience left me laughing, nodding in agreement, or reflective. I appreciated how he tackled common situations or dilemmas without resorting to dramatic descriptions or contrived humor to share what was, in many cases, a universal moral truth.

One of my favorite essays was "Sleight of Hand," in which Greenberg described his daily encounters with a down-and-out employee at the local coffee shop. The clerk began to undercharge Greenberg in hopes he would toss the savings into his tip jar. Greenberg's masterful retelling of how this tested each of their character cores was fast-paced and engaging until the last sentence with its moment of truth. In fact, one of Greenberg's trademarks is the zinger of a closing sentence.

Greenberg was brutally honest in the essay "$493 in Singles and Fives," about how his own family made their monetary fortune in American society through the selling of scrap metal. When his father's brother gave him—a poor, struggling writer—his "pocket change," an internal conflict developed within Greenberg about how people earn a living:

> The bills were almost untouchable—Ellie had been incontinent—yet without hesitation I stuffed them, reeking and soiled, in my pockets. I returned to my apartment.... my need for (the money) was a mockery of my attempts to transcend what I regarded as my family's grasping, immigrant-minded ways. Yet in a crisscross of logic, my very desire for the money drove me to hand it over to my father. As a grown man my father sometimes came home from the family's scrap-metal yard with blood dribbling out of the corner of his mouth where my grandfather had slugged him. They fought over the business that had lifted them out of the slums. Was it because it had been so scarce that money brought its new version of misery?

Americana painter Norman Rockwell used to say that when a painting was going bad, he added a dog. Greenberg didn't need to add a dog story, but I'm glad he did with "Dachshund." In this essay, he told of the unenviable job of finding a new home for his miniature wire-haired dachshund, which the breeder had described as "a cross between Truman Capote and Norman Mailer." That alone is funny, but the essay gets even funnier when the new prospective owner reveals her concern that the astrological sign of the dog—and of Greenberg—doesn't work well with her own star sign. Ultimately, it was Greenberg's humor that won me over hands down in favor this collection. It will win you over too.

Five Kingdoms
by Kelle Groom
Anhinga Press, 2010
106 pages
$15.00 (paper)

Reviewed by Karissa Knox Sorrell

Kelle Groom's third book of poetry hauntingly examines how the five kingdoms of living things interact with each other across time and space. Her poems span the globe and the history of Earth, from a three-million-year-old skeleton in Ethiopia to a White House conference with Jeb Bush in Tampa. In the poem "Oldest Map of the World" Groom insists that history, place, and humans are superimposed on each other:

> *and here we found the first map of the world, made of clay,*
> *so small, it fits in the palm of a hand,*
> *the Euphrates emptying into your wrist,*
> *and to the north, fingers shade triangles of mountains.*

As the human soul journeys toward meaning, it interprets the world without the boundaries of time. "I feel like a person / who woke up in the future, / and it looked like an old / photograph of the city," Groom tells us. In the poem "Ode to the Year 600" we are transported to a seventh-century graveyard in which we feel right at home.

> *I'm no expert on the year 600,*
> *so long ago it seems dark as tobacco,*
> *but I woke there a couple of times,*
> *and there was a lot of room, the air*
> *polished and new, like good silverware . . .*
> *and I can look through*
> *to the sea, touch the stone*
> *wall like tapping a shoulder.*

These poems remind us that though humans are mortal, their imprint on the Earth is eternal. The first poem, "Bone Built for Eternity", an ekphrastic poem based on the artwork of Guillermo Kuitca, says,

that even if you are buried
for three million years,
your body nearly hidden in stone,
we will come looking
for you.

In "Newgrange", the lens of archaeology and architecture renders the curtain between the living and the dead translucent: "Do you remember the years before / the pyramids? We were always stacking / stones to guide the soul in and out." Groom transforms Newgrange, an ancient tomb in Ireland, into a safe haven for people on both side of the divide:

here is a place,
and a window that lets the light
unroll like a rug down the aisle to these
stone seats where they can sit among us,
sun on their faces and their cold hands.

Groom does not stop with the idea of human resurrection; her poems are a call to recognize the necessity of all life on earth. "Count all the living things," she commands in the poem "Five Kingdoms". A wounded duck, a SIDS baby, and a girl run over by a tank in Fallujah cause sorrow and remind us of the incomparable worth of all organisms. The balance that must exist on Earth exists in these poems as the merging of human, animal, plant, and element. In one poem, a girl is "barnacled / around a boy on a bike, flashing / like a school of fish by your side." In another, the speaker has become much more than a beekeeper:

bees are buzzing inside, electric
marbles tingling my tongue, lips,
and when I speak, they leave my mouth
instead of words: I write with bees, even
draw in bee.

While that speaker deals with fear, another speaker confronts the social forces that separate people, saying, "I wanted to walk / toward her, but others rose up between us like the sea." In Groom's world, each life rediscovers itself in a reflection of its surroundings.

Don't think that Groom is merely a nature poet, however. She keenly weaves a consciousness of modern culture into these poems. In "Oprah and the Underworld", "Sharon Stone was promoting her girlfight / movie with Halle Berry, but Oprah / / was more interested in Sharon's real- / life head injury." Though the poem hits a comic nerve, it also reiterates the tone of urgency that permeates the book: "Sharon saying how near it all was - / / the nearness of death, waving her hands again, / as if waving hello at Death, another guest." The urgency is the need to save and cherish all life, and Groom's gift is making you want to do so without being preachy.

Camden Blues
By Joe Anthony
Wind Publications
222 Pages
$16.00

Reviewed by James B. Goode

Joe Anthony's second book, a collection of four novellas, five short stories, three poems, and one memoir, showcases his considerable talent for all four genres. This book chronicles the decay of the once mighty industrial city of Camden, New Jersey where his grandfather emigrated from Newfoundland in 1900 following the promise of a good job. *Camden Blues* is a kind of love story about a place that is pretty much done—a celebration of a place that isn't celebrated anymore.

Anthony's look at this microcosm of urban/suburban America is sharp and biting—a kind of love/hate story of the evolution and death or deterioration of the very center of what made this country great. The core of this work is the story of white middle class emigrants living in the cities and suburbs of industrial America in the 1960s and 1970s who are experiencing a sense of displacement, alienation, change and loss. Eventually, they become almost invisible, some fleeing to the larger urban areas like New York City in search of jobs and others staying behind to misplace blame for the malaise of white suburbia on minorities moving in to fill the void. But, larger religious, social, political, and economic forces, often beyond anybody's ability to understand or control, are the real causes of loss and misery in these stories.

Anthony satirizes the religious, political, and social organizations that want to control people. In particular, religious organizations with their trademark rigidity and pursuit of perfection create conflict for the emerging changeable and fallible young people who are struggling with their beliefs. Jews, Catholics, Baptists, Episcopalians, Presbyterians, Methodists, Scientologists, Jehovah Witnesses, and Hare Krishna's are placed under Anthony's microscope in this witty and insightful look into a landscape where some people are so fickle they change religions because of where the bus line more conveniently runs while others stubbornly and unwisely resist change. A whole "cottage industry of salvation" has sprung up in the cities which host a kind of patchwork of evangelicals who vie for lost souls: "They all had one thing in common with the Witnesses: they possessed the truth, and they were prepared to spread it through the world . . ."

Anthony has a great ear for making dialogue natural—for capturing how people actually talk. For example, in the novella "Father Gallagher," the aging protagonist Mary Margaret Brooks talks to her sister about the newly arrived dashing young parish priest Father Gallagher:

> I said to my sister Agnes, "A priest just shouldn't be that good looking." That black curly hair, those blue eyes. And didn't he know it. I'm an old woman and way past all that nonsense, but Jesus, Mary, Joseph, he even fluttered me . . .
> Those kind of looks are like carrying around a loaded gun I said to her.
> "He carries a loaded gun?" Agnes says to me . . . she's my only sister, but the Lord surely misplaced a few cards when he dealt her deck.
> "No," I say patiently. . . I mean his good looks might make something happen that he didn't want to happen." But it's like talking to a two year old. Agnes just looks at me blank like she doesn't have any idea what I'm talking about . . . How she ever had seven children are seven more mysteries I think the church should include along with the Immaculate Conception. Which for all Agnes knows, they probably were.

John Cheever once said, "For me, a page of good prose is where one hears the rain and the noise of battle. . ." In Camden Blues, Joe Anthony has written many good pages of prose that will bring readers to hear the rain and the noise of battle within these deteriorating cities and suburbs. This collection succeeds in not only allowing readers to experience the blues from the loss and transformation that has been felt by Camden, N.J., but to realize that these blues are pandemic—a sad song of woes that a large portion of the population in the United States has heard.

Girl Trouble
by Holly Goddard Jones
Harper Perennial, 2009
368 pages
$14.99 (paper)

Reviewed by Richard Thomas

In her debut collection of short stories, *Girl Trouble*, Holly Goddard Jones touches on many subjects that speak to us all—loss, betrayal, death, and love—and holds nothing back in her portrayal of southern life, or life in general. She does not shy away from darker matter such as rape and murder, but instead, holds the camera steady.

The eight short stories in *Girl Trouble* do several things well: they hook you right away with their opening lines; they maintain tension and drama throughout; and they end with a powerful resonance, be it a whisper or a scream. Take the opening paragraph from "Parts," quite possibly the best story in the collection:

> *I had a daughter. When she was eleven, my husband and I took her to Spring Aces, the local pool park, for swimming lessons. She wore a purple bathing suit, the bikini I allowed over Art's grumbled protests, and she bounced on the diving board a little, and leaped, and cannonballed right into the deep end. The splash of blue-tinted water made a fragile shell around her, gorgeous, and then she went under. She was fearless. There was that moment a mother feels when the heart pauses and the throat goes dry, that fear of—or desire for, maybe—the moment of crisis, when everything changes and you have to change, too, to make sense of it all.*

The key is the opening line, "I *had* a daughter," in the past tense. Setting the stage is one of Jones' strengths—creating tension, hinting at something darker underneath it all, preparing us for the worst possible thing imaginable to come true.

The stories in *Girl Trouble* feel connected, as if they were family, not just a nuclear family, but an extended family including doting aunts, strange uncles and kissing cousins. Jones is happy to keep the closet open to skeletons, revealing dysfunction in all of its mesmerizing and brutal honesty. In "Life Expectancy," a high-school basketball coach commits adultery with one of the girls he coaches. In "Allegory of a Cave," a father makes an awkward attempt to connect with his son, even though the knowledge he tries to pass on could scar the boy for life. In "An Upright Man," a young man betrays a friend, which forces him to grow up too fast and move on from his life in a small town. Jones does not demean small town life. Rather, she reveals the consequences of universal weaknesses such as jealousy, paranoia and lust, which are often harsh and everlasting.

Jones has evolved under the tutelage of Lee K. Abbott, who said "character is what we are in the dark." In the connected stories "Parts" and "Proof," Jones explores the same crime from two angles—that of the killers and that of their prey. She turns a sharp eye to what is left of both criminals and victims after the dust has settled, the shells and husks of their scarred lives littering the gravel roads. Jones' work also owes a debt to the narrative hooks and southern lore of Ron Rash; the darkness and emotion of William Gay; and the perspective of Flannery O'Connor.

Holly Goddard Jones is obviously a very talented emerging author. *Girl Trouble* represents a great opportunity to get in on the ground floor with her powerful language, visceral imagery and startling revelations.

Leviathan
by Scott Westerfeld
Simon Pulse, 2009
440 pages
$20.00

Reviewed by Matt Markgraf

In the throes of The Great War, British Darwinists descend into Clanker German territory with airships fabricated from living-breathing tissue. The Clankers retaliate with an arsenal of steam-driven ironclad walking machines. Alek, the young prince of the Austro-Hungarian Empire is forced to flee his homeland after his parents' assassination. Meanwhile Deryn, a girl disguised as a boy, joins the British Air Service in honor of her father, a recently deceased airman. Here's where the first book in Scott Westerfeld's epic young adult trilogy *Leviathan* begins.

In *How to Write and Publish a Successful Young Adult Novel*, author Regina Brooks defines a "literary work" as something that is character-driven, rather than plot driven. By designing separate chapters for Alek and Deryn, Westerfeld delivers not one, but two character-driven perspectives. Thus, before Alek and Deryn even meet, readers understand the delicate tension that carries the weight of the story. These two perspectives inevitably converge in a masterful scene of desperation and diplomacy.

The plot is really quite simple: airship breaks down, and with some assistance the airship starts up again. The story's emotional weight is hinged on the relationship of the unlikely duo, Alek and Deryn, but much of the text is spent in vivid description of how the whale-like airship realistically functions and how exactly the robots engage in combat. Through these details, Westerfeld strikes a fine balance in defining an avant-garde world and humanizing its inhabitants, thus making it possible—even believable—that his young heroes can put and end to WWI.

Westerfeld's descriptions of settings, scenes and creatures succeed in terms of credibility. Here's his account of Deryn's first flight in a Huxley (a small, living air-balloon affixed with a swing-like seat): "Deryn looked up and saw the medusa's body alight with the sunrise, pulsing veins and arteries running like iridescent ivy through its translucent flesh. The tentacles drifted in the soft breezes around her, capturing pollen and insects and sucking them into the stomach sack above." I never questioned the plausibility of the Huxley because Westerfeld makes it seem as if Huxleys had always existed. Here's his account of a creature processing hydrogen: "It should have been nauseating, Deryn supposed, hanging suspended from all those gaseous dead insects. Or terrifying, with nothing but a few leather straps between her and a quarter mile of tumbling to a terrible death. But she felt as grand as an eagle on the wing." In this scene, the reader flies terrified and exhilarated along with Deryn over the city below.

Leviathan is inspiring in its ambition. The steampunk sub-genre can easily fall into the trap of being gimmicky, over-embellishing its artistic flair, but instead Westerfeld succeeds by going for measured practicality and pacing. For anyone who wants a character-centric, rollicking fun read in the realm of young adult fiction, I highly recommend Scott Westerfeld's *Leviathan*. I must advise you, however, that it is the first book in a trilogy. Its ending will make you immediately want to pick up the next book, which is due to be published this autumn.

Contributors' Notes

Gina Barnard has published in *Web Del Sol*, *Poetry Now*, *Cosumnes River Review*, and in Japanese translation in *Poemaholic Café* (Tsukuba, Japan). She is currently an editorial assistant for *Poetry International*. She was born in Fussa, Tokyo, grew up (mostly) in the Sacramento Valley, and lives in San Diego, California.

Before retiring, **Michael Cohen** wrote academic books: his last was *Murder Most Fair: The Appeal of Mystery Fiction* published in 2000 by Fairleigh Dickinson University Press. Now he writes personal essays, two of which are forthcoming in *North Dakota Quarterly* and *The Kenyon Review*. He and his wife Katharine live on Kentucky Lake when they're not in the Tucson Mountains.

Michael Copperman teaches writing at the University of Oregon, where he earned his MFA in fiction. His nonfiction has appeared in *The Oxford American*, *GOOD*, *Guernica*, *Creative Nonfiction*, *Teachers and Writers*, *Stanford Magazine*, *Post Road*, *Anderbo*, *Brevity*, *The Oregonian*, *The Register-Guard*, and *The Eugene Weekly*. His fiction has been published in the Munster Literature Centre's journal *Southword*, *The Arkansas Review*, and *34th Parallel*. He was the recipient of the 2009 Walter Morey Fellowship from Oregon Literary Arts.

Todd Davis is the author of *The Least of These*, published in 2010 by Michigan State University Press, *Some Heaven*, published in 2007 by Michigan State University Press, and *Ripe*, published in 2002 by Bottom Dog Press. He's also co-editor of *Making Poems: 40 Poems with Commentary by the Poets*, SUNY Press 2010. His poetry has been featured on the radio by Garrison Keillor on *The Writer's Almanac* and by Ted Kooser in his syndicated newspaper column *American Life in Poetry*. His recent work can be found in *Shenandoah*, *Poetry East*, *West Branch*, *River Styx*, *Atlanta Review*, *Sou'Wester*, and *Nimrod*.

Angela Delarmente was born near a volcano in the Philippines, and grew up in California and Japan. She currently lives in the Midwest where she is an MFA candidate at the University of Wisconsin-Madison. She is working on a collection of short stories from which "Crash Zoom" appears, and will soon head west to Seattle, Washington.

Brett Foster has work in or forthcoming in *Image*, *The Kenyon Review*, *Pleiades*, *Poetry East*, *Raritan*, and *Seattle Review*. Northwestern University Press will publish his first poetry collection *The Garbage Eater* in 2011. He teaches Renaissance literature and creative writing at Wheaton College, and is also preparing a selected volume of the sonnets of Cecco Angiolieri, a rival of Dante.

Stephen Gibson is the author of the poetry collections *Masaccio's Expulsion* and *Rorschach Art*. His third collection, *Frescoes*, won the 2009 Idaho Prize for Poetry and was recently released by Lost Horse Press. His latest collection, *Paradise*, a finalist for the Miller Williams Arkansas Poetry Prize, will be published by the University of Arkansas Press in 2011.

Anne Haines is the author of the chapbook *Breach*, published in 2008 by Finishing Line Press. Her poems have appeared in *Field*, *diode* and *Bloom*, among others. She is currently working on a manuscript of poems about a fictional rock musician tentatively titled *Chasing Angels*, from which "The Roar the Day After" is taken. She lives in Bloomington, Indiana, where she serves as the website editor for the Indiana University Libraries.

Christine Hale has contributed to *Saw Palm*, *Arts & Letters*, *Apalachee Review*, and *Natural Bridge*. Her debut novel is *Basil's Dream*, published in 2009 by Livingston Press. A fellow of MacDowell, Ucross, Hedgebrook, and the Virginia Center for the Creative Arts, Ms. Hale has been a finalist for the Glimmer Train Short Story Award for New Writers and the Rona Jaffe Foundation Writers' Award. She teaches in the Murray State University Low-Residency MFA Program as well as the Great Smokies Writing Program in Asheville, North Carolina.

John Kay is both a poet and a photo-artist living in Germany. His poems and photographs have been published in the *Cortland Review*, *Bellevue Lit Review*, *Pearl*, *5AM*, the *New York Quarterly*, and others. He has three chapbooks and a new book titled *Phantom of the Apple*, forthcoming from Beginner's Mind Press.

Sandra Kohler is the author of a new collection of poems titled *Improbable Music*, forthcoming in 2011 from Word Press. Her previous collections include *The Ceremonies of Longing*, winner of the 2002 AWP Award Series in Poetry and subsequently published by the University of Pittsburgh Press, and *The Country of Women*, published in 1995 by Calyx Books. Her poems have appeared in *Prairie Schooner*, *The New Republic*, *Beloit Poetry Journal*, *The Gettysburg Review*, *The Southern Review*, and *Colorado Review*.

Sandy Longhorn is the author of *Blood Almanac*, published in 2006 by Anhinga Press. Prior to its publication, the collection won the 2005 Anhinga Prize for Poetry. Her work has also appeared in or is forthcoming in *The American Poetry Journal, The Collagist, Connotation Press*, and *Juked*. Her numerous accomplishments include an Individual Artist Fellowship from the Arkansas Arts Council.

Beth Lordan is the author of *August Heat*, a novel published in 1987 by Harper & Row, *And Both Shall Row*, a collection of short stories published in 1998 by Picador, and *But Come Ye Back*, a novel in stories published by William Morrow in 2004. Her short fiction has appeared in *Farmers Market, The Gettysburg Review, The Atlantic Monthly, O.Henry Prize Stories*, and *Best American Short Stories*, and has won prizes from the New York State Council on the Arts and the Illinois Arts Council. She earned her BA and MFA from Cornell University, and presently serves on the faculty of Southern Illinois University Carbondale, where she teaches fiction workshops and forms courses, and directs Irish and Irish Immigration Studies.

Ed McClanahan is a former Wallace Stegner Fellow and author of several books, including *The Natural Man*, *Famous People I Have Known*, and most recently *O the Clear Moment*. His work has appeared in *Esquire*, *Rolling Stone*, and *Playboy*—he twice won *Playboy's* Best Non-Fiction award. He was born in 1932 in Brooksville, Kentucky, and grew up there and in nearby Maysville. A graduate of Miami University (BA) and the University of Kentucky (MA), he has taught writing and English at Stanford, the University of Montana, the University of Kentucky, and elsewhere. McClanahan and his wife Hilda live in Lexington. (Portions of "The Essentials of Western Civilization" appeared previously in *Ace Weekly* and *Open 24 Hours*. An earlier version of the story's opening section supplied the title for McClanahan's 1998 collection *My Vita, if You Will*.)

Julie L. Moore is the author of *Slipping Out of Bloom*, published by WordTech Editions, and *Election Day*, published by Finishing Line Press. A Pushcart Prize nominee, Moore is the recipient of the Rosine Offen Memorial Award from the Free Lunch Arts Alliance, the Janet B. McCabe Poetry Prize from *Ruminate*, and the Judson Jerome Poetry Scholarship from the Antioch Writers' Workshop. Her work has appeared in *Alaska Quarterly Review*, *Atlanta Review*, *Cimarron Review*, *The Southern Review*, and *Valparaiso Poetry Review*.

Chigozie John Obioma was born in Nigeria in 1986. His fiction has appeared in various online journals, and his young adult novel *The Native Hurricane* was published in 2008 by Athena Press, UK. He is currently studying and living in the nation of Cyprus.

Born and raised in Dublin, **Martin Roper** is the author of *Gone*, a portion of which appeared in *The New Yorker*. Roper earned his MFA from the University of Iowa, and is the director of the University of Iowa's Irish Writing Program in Dublin. Most recently he was named the Nancy and Rayburn Watkins Endowed Visiting Professor of Creative Writing at Murray State University.

William Trowbridge is the author of five poetry collections: *Enter Dark Stranger, O Paradise, Flickers, The Complete Book of Kong*, and the forthcoming *Ship of Fool*. His poems have appeared in such periodicals as *The Gettysburg Review, The Iowa Review, The Georgia Review, Poetry, Boulevard,* and *New Letters*. He lives in the Kansas City area and teaches in the University of Nebraska low-residency MFA in writing program.

Avra Wing is the author of the novel *Angie, I Says*, which was made into the film *Angie* starring Geena Davis and James Gandolfini. Most recently her poems have appeared in *Apple Valley Review*, and are slated for the summer issues of *Tattoo Highway* and *Silk Road*. She has also published essays in *The New York Times*, and her memoir, *Doorway on the Mountain*, is currently available at Onlineoriginals.com. Avra is a workshop leader for the New York Writers Coalition, and is an adjunct professor of English at Kingsborough Community College in Brooklyn, New York, where she lives.

Melissa Scholes Young is a writer, mother, teacher, pathological reader, Pushcart Prize nominee and professional juggler, in the metaphorical sense. Her work has been published in *Mothering, Literary Mama, Mused*, and *Yalobusha Review*. She's contributed to the anthologies *A Cup of Comfort for Teachers* and the *Voices of* series from LaChance Publishing. Melissa is currently pursuing an MFA in fiction at Southern Illinois University.

REVIEWERS

Christine Bailey teaches written composition at Union University in Jackson, Tennessee and is completing a novel for young adults.

James B. Goode is professor of English at Bluegrass Community & Technical College and is a poet, essayist, and short story writer. His work has appeared in *The South Carolina Review, Appalachian Journal, Huron Review, Appalachian Heritage*, and *Cape Rock Journal*.

Jacqueline J. Kohl teaches arts and humanities at a private school in central Kentucky. She maintains a piano studio and writes freelance articles for one of her favorite fields, health and nutrition.

Matt Markgraf is an award-winning web developer and late night music host for WKMS, western Kentucky's affiliate of National Public Radio. He is currently completing a young adult novel titled *Mojo's Tiki Lounge*, in which a boy finds himself an unlikely hero on a mysterious tropical island.

A.J. Morgan lived in Alaska for eleven years. There, her favorite job was working on the Mendenhall glacier. She has earned degrees in anthropology, chemistry, and recently an MFA in creative writing. Currently she lives near the Ohio River, and has moved her Russian authors to the top shelf in case it floods.

Karissa Knox Sorrell lives in Gallatin, Tennessee and teaches English as a Second Language. Her poems have been published or are forthcoming in *Relief: A Christian Literary Expression, touchstone, Number One*, and *Etchings*.

Richard Thomas won the 2009 ChiZine Publications Enter the World of *Filaria* contest, and his work is forthcoming or available in *Murky Depths, 3:AM, Dogmatika, Word Riot, Opium*, and *Vain,* as well as in the anthologies *Shivers VI* and *Eternal Night*. His debut novel *Transubstantiate*, a neo-noir thriller, comes out in 2010.

About the Artist
Robert Dafford

Robert Dafford, a native of Lafayette Louisiana, has been designing and painting outdoor works professionally since 1970. He is one of the most prolific and successful muralists in America, with over 350 large-scale public works completed throughout the United States, and also in France, Belgium, England, and Canada.

Dafford's work has been featured or mentioned in *Smithsonian*, *National Geographic*, and *Southern Living* magazines, as well as *The New York Times*, *The Seattle Times*, *Los Angeles Times*, *Ottawa Sun*, *Le Droit*, and countless other venues.

His honors include the Bronze Medaille d'Honneur de la Suresnes in Suresenes (Paris) France for "Horizon," a mural series of violins flying through several countries, representing the power of music and art to break through barriers of language and politics, and a silver medal from the city of Nantes, France for his mural "Departure des Acadians pour Nouvelle Orleans 1768," a 14' x 40' painting twinned with the 12' x 30' "Arrival of the Acadians" at the memorial Monument des Acadians in St. Martinville, Louisiana.

Over a span of almost thirty years, Dafford has painted twenty large-scale canvasses depicting the Expulsion of the Acadians from Acadie (now Nova Scotia) in 1765, leading to their settlement in Louisiana, where they are now known as the Cajuns. Reproductions of these paintings have been used in numerous textbooks, articles, books, and in film and video productions by such groups as BBC, CBC, PBS, History Channel and others.

Though Dafford is known as an historical painter who produces sweeping outdoor murals, he has also created many large-scale paintings for museums, libraries, city halls, churches, homes and other interiors. In the next phase of his career, he plans to focus increasingly on more refined, interior permanent pieces.

COVER ART

From Paducah "Wall to Wall," Portraits from Paducah's Past
Robert Dafford Murals

Front Cover: **George Rogers Clark**

George Rogers Clark (1752-1818), a Virginia surveyor, came to Kentucky to seek his fortune. He thwarted the claim of Richard Henderson and Daniel Boone to the territory west of the Appalachians in 1776 by persuading the Virginia legislature to create Kentucky County. In 1778, Governor Patrick Henry ordered Lieutenant Colonel Clark to attack British posts along the Ohio River. Clark's command captured the Northwest Territory for Virginia. His conquest included the U.S. territory east of the Mississippi, north of the Ohio, and west of the Appalachians. He was the brother of William Clark of the Lewis and Clark Expedition, and the namesake for many American sites, including Chicago's Clark Street, and Clarksville, Tennessee.

Back Cover: **The First Log Cabin**

In 1884, Robert S. Davis recalled that the first cabin in the Paducah area was about sixteen feet square, erected by the Pore brothers, James and William, in April of 1821. Davis identified four families living at the site at that time. Records in Livingston County affirm that a town called "Pekin" claimed the site. In a letter to his son, William Clark wrote that he chose to re-name Paducah to honor the Padoucas tribe, once quite large but decimated by contact with Europeans. Despite its late start, Paducah soon became the largest city in the region due to the favorable location on the rivers and, later, as the terminus of the New Orleans and Ohio Railroad which was connected to lines running south in 1860.

Robert painting a Shawnee village in Point Pleasant, West Virginia (Photo by Lil Elston)

visit us online www.poetryinternational.sdsu.edu

John Ashbery
Jorge Luis Borges
Kamau Brathwaite
Toi Derricotte
Marilyn Hacker
Seamus Heaney
Li-Young Lee
Philip Levine
Ewa Lipska
Osip Mandelstam
Dunya Mikhail

an annual journal of
poetry & translation
from around the world

Poetry International

Ý Nhi
Marge Piercy
Octavio Paz
Adrienne Rich
Luis Omar Salinas
Charles Simic
Gerald Stern
Gary Soto
Marina Tsvetaeva
Derek Walcott
Amir Saadi Youssef

send 3-5 poems of your best work to
Department of English
and Comparative Literature
San Diego State University
500 Campanile Dr.
San Diego, CA 92182-6020